Treasures from the Original

Treasures from the Original

by

Harold J. Berry

MOODY PRESS

CHICAGO

Originally published as *Gems from the Original, Vol. 1.*

Library of Congress Cataloging in Publication Data

Berry, Harold J., 1934-
    Treasures from the original.

    "Originally published as Gems from the original,
vol. 1" — T.p. verso.
    Bibliography: p.
    Includes indexes.
    1.Greek language, Biblical — Semantics.
2. Christian life — 1960-   . I. Title.
PA875.B47   1985   225.4'8   85-18755
ISBN 0-8024-2956-4 (pbk.)

1 2 3 4 5 6 7 Printing/VI/Year 90 89 88 87 86 85

Printed in the United States of America

To my wife,

Donna

Together, we have been:
Marriage partners since college days
Parents of Stephen and Deborah since seminary days
Co-workers in the cause of Christ
Companions down the path of life

Contents

CHAPTER   PAGE

Foreword... ix
1. The Believer's Old Nature... 1
2. Power: Ability or Authority?.. 4
3. Sin: Habitual or Occasional?.. 7
4. Reprove: Accuse or Convict?... 11
5. Binding What Is Already Bound 14
6. Which Hell Is Eternal?... 17
7. Temple: Sacred Place or Inner Sanctuary? 21
8. Form: Inner or Outer? 24
9. Submission 26
10. God's Wrath 29
11. The Great Commission... 32
12. A Savior Is Born... 35
13. Praying Without Ceasing 38
14. Dead or Alive?.. 41
15. Testing: For Good or Evil?.. 45
16. A Decision or a Feeling?... 48
17. Perfect: Sinless Perfection or Spiritual Maturity? 51
18. Restoring a Spiritual Brother.. 53
19. Negative Commands... 56
20. A Condition or an Assumption? 59

21. Indifferent Following or Intense Pursuit? 62
22. Is Lust Always Bad? 65
23. Paid in Full 67
24. Appearance of Evil.. 70
25. Kinds of Love 72
26. The Believer's Title Deed 75
27. The Believer's Help 77
28. Ransomed Forever 80
29. Yield! 83
30. Hospitality... 86
31. Does God Punish Believers? 88
32. Needed: More Mimics....................................... 91
33. Building Spiritual Houses.................................. 93
34. Is Fear from God? 97
35. Peace: God's Umpire.. 100
36. Persistence Isn't Enough................................... 102
37. God's Justice Satisfied 105
38. The Conflict of Faith....................................... 108
39. Digging Your Own Treasures 111
    Recommended Tools 115
    Scripture Index... 119
    Greek Word Index 123
    New American Standard Bible Word Index 124

Foreword

God, in His infinite wisdom, used Alexander the Great to bring about the universality of the Greek language. This language, with its fine shades of meaning, was then used by God as He inspired the New Testament writings, which could be understood by the common man of that time. Those today who do not know New Testament Greek can praise the Lord for those who have studied it and who seek to communicate its meaning to others.

Realizing the need for people to understand the marvelous depths of the New Testament, the *Good News Broadcaster* began a column entitled "Gems from the Original," written by Harold J. Berry.

The purpose was not to give an exhaustive treatment of any particular problem, but to show the riches of the Greek New Testament and to provide spiritual food and help to those who study the Bible.

Many readers found this column to be very helpful and asked to have the articles put in book form. *Treasures from the Original* is the result. Each chapter was a separate article when the material appeared in the *Good News Broadcaster*. We are pleased to give these articles a wider distribution by now publishing them in book form.

Harold J. Berry was associated with Back to the Bible for nearly seventeen years. During half of that time he was my personal editorial assistant. In this capacity he conducted several major research projects for me, especially utilizing his wealth of knowledge of the Greek language.

I can therefore highly recommend this book. I am sure that it will be a blessing; but even more, it will be a help to you in understanding many of the intricate details of meaning in the original and will be a treasure for those who use it properly.

Theodore H. Epp
Founding Director
Back to the Bible

1

The Believer's Old Nature

Since the New Testament was first written in the Greek language, it is especially intriguing to go back beyond our translations to see some of the fine shades of meaning in the original words. Rarely does the proper use of the Greek word completely change the meaning that we have in our translations, but it often makes the thought more forceful and draws the doctrinal distinctions even finer.

One word that does this is *katargeō*, which appears twenty-seven times in the Greek New Testament. The basic meaning of *katargeō* is "to make idle or inactive." It is also used in the sense of "to render inoperative" — or, as we might say, "to put out of commission."

This word occurs once in both Luke and Hebrews and all other times in Paul's epistles. A significant use of this word is in Romans 6:6 where it is translated "destroyed" (KJV*); "rendered powerless" (NIV†); and "done away with" (NASB‡). The entire verse reads: "Knowing this, that our old self was crucified with Him,

* King James Version.
† *New International Version.*
‡ *New American Standard Bible.*

that our body of sin might be done away with, that we should no longer be slaves to sin." A proper understanding of the word is essential in this passage if one is to know the true relationship of the old self-life dominated by the old nature. There are two extremes of Christian thinking involved: some think the old nature still has such a death grip on them that they cannot effectively serve Christ; others think the old nature was completely eradicated when they received Christ and that they no longer commit any sin.

The same word *(katargeō)* is translated "nullify" in Romans 3:3, where the apostle asks, "What then? If some did not believe, their unbelief will not nullify the faithfulness of God, will it?" The thought here is that just because some people do not believe in God, that does not negate His faithfulness. Paul states the same truth another way in 2 Timothy 2:13: "If we are faithless, He remains faithful; for He cannot deny Himself."

Katargeō appears twice in 1 Corinthians 13:8. This verse states: "Love never fails; but if there are gifts of prophecy, they will be done away *(katargeō)*; if there are tongues, they will cease; if there is knowledge, it will be done away *(katargeō)*."

Although the NASB consistently translates both occurrences of *katargeō* as "done away," it is interesting that the KJV translates the first as "fail" and the second as "vanish away." The NIV translates the first as "cease" and the second as "pass away."

Contention had arisen in the Corinthian church over gifts. This church did not lack any of the gifts (1:7), and yet the believers were not spiritual but carnal (3:1). In 1 Corinthians 13 Paul instructs the believers in the proper way to use their gifts — in love. In order to establish the superiority of love, the apostle reminds them that there would come a time when the gifts of prophecy and knowledge would be rendered inoperative or done away, but love will always continue in its importance. Verse 10 of this same passage affirms that "but when the perfect comes, the partial will be done away." Here the word *katargeō* is translated "done away." That which is in part is not done away with in the sense of being destroyed, but the partial is no longer necessary when that which is complete is present.

In the light of the above, it is evident in Romans 6 that the sin nature was not destroyed; rather, it was done away with in the sense that it was rendered inoperative. It is like an electronic radio that is unplugged; it is not destroyed, but its power has been broken. Though the power of the old nature over the believer is broken, he is still able to put it back into operation by yielding to its desires.

The conflict within every believer, therefore, is whether to yield to the new nature he has because he is in Christ or to the old nature with its self-desires. In Galatians 5:16 Paul says, "Walk in the Spirit, and you will not carry out the desire of the flesh."

The believer is to yield to the Spirit, not to the flesh. When the believer commits an act of sin, he breaks his fellowship with the Spirit. The believer's remedy for broken fellowship is found in 1 John 1:9: "If we confess our sins, He is faithful and righteous to forgive us our sins and to cleanse us from all unrighteousness." When the Christian confesses his sin, God forgives his disobedience, and once again the fruit of the Spirit is manifested through his life. Yielding to the desires of the flesh will result in the manifestation of the works of the flesh, but walking by means of the Spirit will result in the manifestation of the fruit of the Spirit.

The person who has received Christ as Savior is no longer in bondage to the power of the old nature. Christ broke the power of sin through His death on the cross. Though each believer is delivered from the power of sin, he is still capable of sinning by choosing to yield to the desires of the flesh. All believers may look forward to that day when Christ will return to deliver His own from the very presence of sin by taking them to be with Himself.

2

Power: Ability or Authority?

There are six words in the Greek New Testament that are translated "power" in various English translations. The two principal words are *dunamis* and *exousia*. Although the word "power" is not necessarily a bad translation for either of these words, it is at least apparent that since they are different words, they must emphasize different aspects of power. When one learns the special emphasis of each word, the New Testament will take on an even richer meaning.

"Power" may be used in speaking of a football player who is a rock-hard two hundred pounds and is able to drive through the middle of the defensive line. Or "power" may be used to convey the idea of authority — a policeman has power because he has authority vested in him by his government, but his power is not greater than the authority given to him by his superiors.

The word *dunamis* — which occurs more than one hundred times in the Greek New Testament — emphasizes power in the sense of "ability," though it does not always stress that aspect of power. The use of the word *dunamis* to emphasize ability is seen in 2 Corinthians 8:3: "For I testify that according to their ability, and beyond their ability they gave of their own accord." The Corinthians gave of their finances according to their ability or means after they had first given themselves to the Lord. Their power to give was their ability to give.

The word *dunamis* is also used in the New Testament in assuring the Christian that God is responsible for keeping him: "Who are protected by the power of God through faith for a salvation ready to be revealed in the last time" (1 Peter 1:5). There is no question that God has the authority to keep the believer secure; however, that which is stressed in this verse is that the believer is protected by the ability of God. Because God is omnipotent, the believer never needs to be concerned that God may not have enough ability to keep him secure.

Perhaps one of the most significant verses where *dunamis* occurs as far as the Christian is concerned is Acts 1:8: "But you shall receive power when the Holy Spirit has come upon you; and you shall be My witnesses both in Jerusalem, and in all Judea and Samaria, and even to the remotest part of the earth." Before ascending to the Father, Christ assured the believers that they would have power to witness after the Holy Spirit came into their lives. While it is true that the believer can witness with authority because he knows Christ as Savior, the greatest concern voiced by the average Christian is that he might have the ability to witness. Because Acts 1:8 uses the word *dunamis* for "power," it is clear that Christ was stressing to the believers that the *ability* to witness would be theirs after the coming of the Holy Spirit into their lives.

A synonym for *dunamis* is *exousia,* which also appears more than one hundred times in the Greek New Testament. The primary meaning of *exousia* is the "power of choice" or "liberty of action." In New Testament times, *exousia* was commonly used in wills and contracts to denote the "claim" or "right" that one had over something.

The primary meaning of *exousia* is seen in 1 Corinthians 9:6: "Or do only Barnabas and I not have a right to refrain from working?" It is obvious in this verse that the apostle Paul was talking about his authority or right to make the decision not to work. Since he and Barnabas were giving their lives to minister to others, they could expect to be supported by those to whom they were ministering. Paul had the authority to make this decision, but he chose to support himself by his own labors so the gospel could be preached without charge.

The word *exousia* is also used in Romans 9:21: "Or does not the potter have a right over the clay, to make from the same lump one vessel for honorable use, and another for common use?" Here it is evident that the potter has the power of choice to decide what he will do with the clay — he has the authority to choose.

One of the most commonly quoted verses where *exousia* appears is John 1:12: "But as many as received Him, to them He gave he the right to become children of God, even to those who believe in His name." It is extremely significant that *exousia,* which stresses right or authority, is used in John 1:12 and not *dunamis,* which emphasizes the ability or means to do something. The Scriptures make clear that no one has the ability in himself to become a child of God, because it is impossible to merit salvation through works: "For by grace you are saved through faith; and that not of your-selves, it is the gift of God; not as a result of works, that no one should boast" (Ephesians 2:8-9). However, the good news is that even though you cannot earn salvation by works, it is your right by the power of choice to become a child of God by receiving Jesus Christ as your personal Savior. This authority is given to you by Jesus Christ Himself, because when you receive Him as Savior, the righteousness of God is imputed, or placed on your account, so that you have a perfect position in Christ. This is not because of your ability but because of what Christ accomplished for you on the cross.

How wonderful it is not only to be children of God by the power of choice but also to have the ability to witness to others as a result of the indwelling Holy Spirit in our lives.

3
Sin: Habitual or Occasional?

Some of the choicest treasures to be discovered in the study of New Testament Greek are found in the tenses of the language.

In English the tense of a verb has to do only with the time of the action — past, present, or future. In Greek there are two important factors in every tense: the time of the action and the kind of action. The kind of action is often more important than the time of action.

The Greek tenses are able to show such things as present continuous action, past continuous action, past complete action with a continuing effect, past action viewed in a single perspective without reference to the limits of the action, and future action that is either continuous or viewed in a single perspective.

All these tenses and their fine shades of meaning are important, and this is especially true of the present tense. In fact, it is almost impossible to understand some passages in the New Testament unless one understands the significance of the present tense. This is particularly true of 1 John 3:6-9.

Some who are unaware of the Greek tenses underlying the translation of this portion in the King James Version have misunderstood what the text is saying. Verse 6 says, "Whosoever abideth in him sinneth not" (KJV); verse 9 says, "Whosoever is born of God doth not commit sin" (KJV). Some have concluded on the basis of these statements that one who is a child of God is sinlessly perfect, but is that what these verses teach?

The Greek present tense emphasizes continuous action in present time. When the Bible student realizes which verbs are in the present tense in 1 John 3:6-9, he is amazed at how easily an otherwise difficult passage can be understood. Verse 6 says, "No one who abides in Him sins; no one who sins has seen Him or knows Him." The verb "sin," used twice in this verse, is in the present tense. Since the present tense emphasizes continuous action, it is evident that this verse is talking about the person who continually sins, or practices sin. Therefore, the one who habitually sins is not abiding in Christ; that is, he has not received Christ as his Savior.

This passage does not support the teaching that the believer never sins. The first epistle of John was written to show Christians the importance of fellowship and to point out the marks of a true Christian. In verse 1 of chapter 2, the apostle John reminds Christians that he wrote these things "that you may not sin." But note that he adds, "And if anyone sins, we have an Advocate with the Father, Jesus Christ the righteous." Although John was writing to help Christians live free from sin, he was aware that they might fall into occasional acts of sin; therefore, he reminded them that Christ was standing by, ready to be their heavenly Advocate if they should happen to sin. This assurance was especially meaningful because John had just told his readers, "If we confess our sins, He is faithful and righteous to forgive us our sins and to cleanse us from all unrighteousness" (1:9).

John also gave this assurance: "Little children, let no one deceive you; the one that practices righteousness is righteous, just as He is righteous" (3:7). The word "practices" in this verse is a translation of the Greek word "do" in the present tense, thus emphasizing a continuous activity. Therefore, the verse stresses that the result of one's being a Christian is that he continuously does righteous acts; that is, he practices righteousness. It is impossible for anyone to habitually do righteous acts unless he is a Christian. When a person receives Christ, the Holy Spirit indwells his life and works out the life of Christ through him. This results in practicing righteousness.

Verse 8 further develops this thought: "The one who practices sin is of the devil; for the devil has sinned from the beginning." Here the verbs "practices" and "sinned" are both in the present tense, which emphasizes continual action.

From verse 6 we learned that whoever practices sin has not known Christ; in verse 8 we discover that such a person really has his origin in the devil. This is never said of a person after he receives Christ as Savior, even though he is capable of committing occasional acts of sin. The one who has placed his faith in Christ has been born again, and his origin is no longer in Satan but in Christ.

Since his fall it has been in Satan's nature to practice sin; but the last part of verse 8 reminds us, "The Son of God appeared for this purpose, that He might destroy the works of the devil."

Verse 9 states one of the most profound truths in the New Testament: "No one who is born of God practices sin." It is impossible to properly interpret this phrase without an awareness of the significance of the Greek present tense — continuous action in present time. The word "practices" is a good translation of the present tense. This verse does not say that a person who is born of God never commits occasional acts of sin, but it does teach that a person who is born of God will not practice sin throughout his life.

The question that naturally arises is, How is it possible to make such an absolute statement about the Christian? The answer is given in the rest of the verse: "Because His seed abides in him; and he cannot sin, because he is born of God." The verb "abides" is also in the present tense. Why is it impossible for a true believer to practice sin, or to habitually sin? Because God's seed continually remains in him.

This is why God can trust the believer to live, without giving him a set of laws such as the Mosaic law. The believer has the righteousness of God credited to him, so he no longer desires to sin. He wants to please God in every aspect; and when he does commit sin, the Holy Spirit convicts him of it. The significant difference between a saved person who sins and an unsaved person who sins is that the saved person is convicted by the indwelling Holy Spirit, but the unsaved person is not.

It is wonderful to realize that when a person receives Christ, he becomes a new creature, and the old things pass away (2 Corinthians 5:17). Therefore, the born-again person no longer habitually does those things that dishonor God, because the indwelling Holy Spirit has changed his desires.

4

Reprove: Accuse or Convict?

Every believer ought to be concerned about how he can have a more effective witness to unsaved people. It is not methods, logic, or rhetoric that actually bring a person to Christ, but the Holy Spirit — He produces the new birth (John 3:5-6). It is obvious, then, that if any Christian is to be successful in introducing others to Christ, he must know how the Holy Spirit works in lives to bring conviction of sin and a desire to know Christ as Savior.

One of the most significant passages in the Bible that give insight into the working of the Holy Spirit in salvation is John 16:7-11. In this passage, which is a part of the Upper Room discourse, Christ tells the disciples that after He has ascended to the Father, He will send another Comforter, or Paraclete, who will be of help to them. This reference is to the Holy Spirit, who later descended on the Day of Pentecost to take up residence in the life of every believer. Christ promised that when the Holy Spirit came, He would reprove the world of sin, of righteousness, and of judgment (v. 8).

But what is it to "convict" the world of these things? To reprove or rebuke does not necessarily mean to convince people they are wrong. A parent may reprove his teenager for staying out too late at night, but this does not mean the young person is really convinced it was wrong. And it is also possible to unjustly rebuke a person when he is really not guilty.

The extent of the Spirit's work is understood from John 16:7-11 when one learns the true meaning of the word "convict." This word is a translation of the Greek word *elegchō,* which appears seventeen times in the New Testament. As *elegchō* was used in New Testament times, it involved conviction that was based on unquestionable proof. It was used in the courts of the day when referring to a person who had been tried and convicted. This word stresses conviction to the extent that there is no doubt in the person's mind but that the one on trial is guilty.

In New Testament usage Christ brought out the force of this word by applying it to Himself. He asked, "Which one of you convicts Me of sin?" (John 8:46). The word translated "convicts" is the word *elegchō.* Christ was able to say that no one convicted Him of sin, because obviously He had no sin (see 1 John 3:5).

On the basis of the true meaning of *elegchō* we see that the Holy Spirit will actually convict, or convince, the world of sin, righteousness, and judgment. It is not that He rebukes and the person remains unconvinced; rather, it is a convincing of the individual of sin, of righteousness, and of judgment.

The question logically arises as to what sin is referred to in this passage. This sin is specified in John 16:9: "Concerning sin, because they do not believe in Me." The sin involved is not various acts of wrongdoing but failure to believe in Jesus Christ.

As we witness to others, we need to emphasize that the reason they are under condemnation is not because of individual acts or habits of sin but because they have refused to place their faith in Jesus Christ as their personal Savior.

Christ also promised that the Holy Spirit would convict the world of righteousness. Not only is it the Spirit's ministry to convince the unsaved person of his sin, He also convinces him that the righteousness of God will be applied to him if he will place his faith in Christ. The unsaved person will probably not be able to express what has happened in this way, but it is the work of the Spirit to convince him that he will be acceptable to God if he places his faith in Christ.

The Holy Spirit also convicts the unsaved of judgment. Notice it is not of a judgment that is coming but of a judgment that is past, for it is the judgment of the "ruler of this world" (v. 11). The "ruler of this world" refers to the same person that 2 Corinthians 4:4 calls the "god of this world." This person is Satan. He has blinded the minds of the unsaved. Satan was judged when Christ died on the cross, though the time of his final execution is yet to come. It is the ministry of the Holy Spirit to convince the unsaved person that sin has been judged at the cross and that he can escape condemnation by placing his faith in Christ.

In the light of these truths in John 16:7-11, the Christian can do no better in his witnessing than to help the unsaved person see what the Holy Spirit is bringing him to see: that he is condemned for his rejection of Jesus Christ, that the righteousness of God will be given to him when he believes (2 Corinthians 5:21), and that his sin has been judged on the cross and he can have eternal life by receiving Christ as Savior.

5
Binding What Is Already Bound

After Peter's confession, "Thou art the Christ, the Son of the living God" (Matthew 16:16), the Lord Jesus Christ said, "I will give you the keys of the kingdom of heaven; and whatever you shall bind on earth shall be bound in heaven, and whatever you shall loose on earth shall be loosed in heaven" (v. 19).

Almost the identical statement was made to the other disciples (Matthew 18:18), so it is obvious that more than Peter were included in this promise. But what is really meant by this statement that has confused so many? In what sense is it true that whatever Peter and the other disciples bound would also be bound in heaven? Does this mean that they had the authority to forgive sin as well as not to forgive sin?

The solution lies in the proper understanding of the Greek tense used in the words "shall bind" and "shall loose." In the discussion of the Greek tenses in chapter 3, it was stressed that there are two factors involved in each Greek tense: the time of the action and the kind of action. As to the time of the action, the Greek perfect tense denotes past time. As to the kind of action, this tense sees it as completed action with continuing effect.

The perfect tense is used in Galatians 2:20, where Paul says, "I have been crucified with Christ." The apostle had already been crucified with Christ because he had previously received Him as Savior. His crucifixion with Christ was a past act, but it had a continuing effect on his life.

The perfect tense is also used in Ephesians 2:8, which says, "For by grace you have been saved through faith." The Ephesian Christians had already been saved by the time of Paul's writing to them, and the effect of their conversion had continued in their lives.

With the significance of the Greek perfect tense in mind, the solution to the problem presented in Matthew 16:19 is not difficult to find. The words "shall bind" and "shall loose" are in the Greek perfect tense. Literally, it is "Whatever you bind on earth shall already have been bound in heaven, and whatever you loose on earth shall already have been loosed in heaven."

In the light of this, what is the meaning intended in Matthew 16:19 and 18:18? Is it not meaningless to bind what is already bound and to loose what is already loosed? There is some support for the idea of understanding the words "bind " and "loose" to be commonly used in rabbinical language for "forbid" and "permit," respectively. If this is intended, the meaning would be that the disciples were to forbid on earth what was already forbidden in heaven and to permit on earth what was already permitted in heaven.

It is perhaps most logical from the context to take the meaning to be that the disciples had the responsibility and privilege of telling others what was true of them as far as God was concerned. The person who refused to place his trust in Christ was still bound by sin, but the person who received Him as Savior was loosed from the bondage of sin. Every Christian can exercise this same prerogative today. If a person has received Christ as Savior, we can assure him he is loosed from sin, because he has already been loosed as far as God is concerned; and we can declare those bound who refuse Christ, because this is already true from God's viewpoint.

These truths also apply to John 20:23, which says, "If you forgive the sins of any, their sins have been forgiven them; if you retain the sins of any, they have been retained." The words "have been forgiven" and "have been retained" are translations of the perfect tense. Therefore, the meaning of this verse is similar to Matthew 16:19 and 18:18. The disciples could declare sins forgiven only if they had already been forgiven in heaven. And they could refuse to forgive the sins of those who had rejected Christ only because in heaven their sins were still unforgiven.

No one but God has the power to forgive sin, and He has never given this power to any man. If any person claims to have this power, he should be reminded that not only is there no scriptural basis for such a claim, but also that this is a false gospel and the curse of God rests on that person: "If any man is preaching to you a gospel contrary to that which you received, let him be accursed" (Galatians 1:9).

What a wonderful privilege it is to tell others about Christ and to tell them they can be loosed from sin's penalty by receiving Christ as Savior!

6

Which Hell Is Eternal?

Much confusion about hell has resulted from the fact that three Greek words are translated by the same English word in the King James Version. The three Greek words are *tartaros, hadēs*, and *geenna,* which are all translated "hell." When most people think of the word "hell," they think of the final destiny of those who reject Christ as Savior. But do all three of these words refer to that place?

The noun *tartaros* does not actually occur in the New Testament, but the verb *(tartaroō)* related to the noun occurs once. The verse is 2 Peter 2:4 where this word is translated "hell" not only by the KJV but also by the NIV and NASB. The verse states: "For if God did not spare the angels when they sinned, but cast them into hell and committed them to pits of darkness, reserved for judgment." The individuals referred to in this verse were not those who had rejected Christ; rather, they were angels who had sinned and who are now reserved for judgment. Therefore, *tartaros* does not refer to "hell" as we commonly think of it; rather, it refers to a place of confinement for these angels until they are judged.

The word *hadēs* appears ten times in the New Testament. It is used by three authors: Matthew, Luke, and John. The word appears twice in Matthew (11:23; 16:18), twice in Luke (10:15; 16:23), twice in Acts (2:27, 31), and four times in Revelation (1:18; 6:8; 20:13, 14). A detailed study of the context of each of these verses provides interesting information about hades, but perhaps the most information in one passage is found in Luke 16:19-31. Questions about what it is like in hades are answered in this passage.

The rich man in hades still retained his senses, for he was fully conscious of the torment through which he was passing. Not only could he feel the torment of hades itself, he was tormented by the thought that his five brothers yet at home would also come to this place. He thought he could prevent them from coming to hades if he could persuade Abraham to send Lazarus to talk to them. But Abraham reminded him that if his five brothers would not pay any attention to Moses and the prophets, they would not be persuaded even if someone who had risen from the dead went to them.

It is apparent that the rich man in hades was not experiencing what some cults refer to as "soul sleep," the supposed unconscious existence of the dead prior to the resurrection of the body. The rich man had all of his faculties and was experiencing extreme torment.

Though there is torment, hades is only a temporary abode for dead unbelievers. Revelation 20:13-15 says that hades will deliver up the dead that are in it, and these people will be judged and then cast into the lake of fire. In the light of this, hades is not the final destiny of those who reject Christ, but it is a place of torment for them until they are resurrected to stand before God at the great white throne judgment. Since hades is not the final destiny of the lost, *hadēs* is another word that does not exactly fit the teaching regarding the place we commonly refer to as "hell."

The other word translated "hell" is *geenna*. This word occurs twelve times in the New Testament and is used by four authors — Matthew, Mark, Luke, and James. *Geenna* occurs seven times in Matthew (5:22, 29, 30; 10:28; 18:9; 23:15, 33), three times in Mark (9:43, 45, 47), once in Luke (12:5), and once in James (3:6).

Six of the twelve references to geenna mention fire as one of its characteristics. Eleven of the twelve references are in the gospels and are the recorded words of the Lord Jesus Christ. But where did the word *geenna* originate?

Southeast of Jerusalem there was a place known as the "valley of Hinnom" (Joshua 15:8). It was also referred to as "Gehenna" from the Hebrew word *ge-hinnom*, which means "valley of Hinnom." During Old Testament times children were offered to Molech in this valley (2 Chronicles 33:1-6; Jeremiah 7:31).

Later, after such heathen practices were stopped, the Jews used the valley to dispose of their rubbish as well as the bodies of dead animals and unburied criminals. To consume all of this, a fire burned continuously, known as the "Gehenna of fire." To be in the "Gehenna of fire" would be the most excruciating torment the human mind could imagine; thus, Christ used this well-known place, with its gnawing worms and burning fires, to teach truths about the unknown place — the final abode of those who reject Him as Savior.

In Mark 9:42-50, the Lord Jesus Christ emphasized that it would be better to lose the most precious things in this life and avoid hell than it would be to retain all that this life holds dear and be cast into hellfire, "where their worm does not die, and the fire is not quenched" (vv. 44, 46, 48).

Geenna is also referred to as the "lake of fire" (Revelation 20:15). Verses 11-15 tell about the great white throne judgment, and here we see that death (where the body has gone) and hades (where the soul has gone) will give up the dead that are in them. The resurrected unbelievers will then stand before the great white throne to be judged according to their works.

This judgment will not be for salvation, because that will already have been decided. It is because these have rejected Christ that they will stand before the great white throne. Apparently this judgment will determine the degree of punishment the unbelievers must endure during their never-ending state of existence. After the judgment, the unbelievers will be cast into the "lake of fire." This is the place Christ had referred to as *geenna*.

Unbelievers are not consumed or annihilated in the lake of fire. This fact is seen by comparing Revelation 19:20 with 20:10. Before the beginning of the thousand-year rule of Christ, two persons, known as the "beast" and "false prophet," will be cast into the lake of fire. After the thousand-year rule of Christ, Satan will also be cast into the lake of fire, and the beast and false prophet will still be there. The unbeliever's punishment for rejecting Christ is spoken of as "eternal punishment" (Matthew 25:46). Thus, *geenna,* not *tartaros* or *hadēs,* refers to the eternal hell.

There are those who object to the teaching about hell, saying that this is not compatible with the biblical teaching about God's love. Since He is a God of love, they argue, it would be impossible for Him to send anyone to such a place.

It is true that Matthew 25:41 says the "eternal fire" was prepared for the devil and his angels. But this same verse makes clear that people will also be cast into this place. The context refers to the judgment of the living Gentiles, and verse 46 shows that the destiny of the unbelievers will be "eternal punishment." Since verse 46 also mentions "eternal life," one cannot logically deny "eternal punishment" without also denying "eternal life."

God is holy and cannot compromise His standards. He is also just and requires that sin must be dealt with. Man's willful sin has separated him from God and has brought him under God's condemnation. Without the intervention of a loving God, no one would be saved from eternal condemnation. But because He is a God of love and is not willing that any should perish (2 Peter 3:9), God sent His only begotten Son to die for the sins of the world (1 John 2:2). Those who receive Christ as Savior are delivered from all condemnation (John 5:24), but those who reject Him will continue in their condemnation throughout all eternity in the lake of fire. Have you received Christ as your Savior?

"For God so loved the world, that He gave His only begotten Son, that whoever believes in Him should not perish, but have eternal life. For God did not send the Son into the world to judge the world, but that the world should be saved through Him. He who believes in Him is not judged; he who does not believe has been judged already, because he has not believed in the name of the only begotten Son of God" (John 3:16-18).

7

Temple: Sacred Place or Inner Sanctuary?

There is a clear distinction drawn in the Scriptures between the Greek words translated "temple." A knowledge of which word is used in a given passage allows some interesting observations to be made about the significance of the events or person involved.

The Greek word *hieron* refers to the entire precincts of a temple, including the outer courts, the porches, and other buildings that were connected with the temple itself. *Hieron* is used seventy one times in the New Testament and always refers to a literal temple. The word is never used in a figurative sense, such as applying it to a person. The word is used almost exclusively in the New Testament to refer to the Temple at Jerusalem, although it was also used to refer to the temple of Diana (Acts 19:27). This shows that there is nothing spiritual in the word itself, as it could be applied to both the Temple of the true God and to the temples of heathen deities. The significance of the word is that it refers to that which is consecrated to deity; therefore, it would refer to the entire temple area regardless of the temple involved.

The other Greek word translated "temple" in the New Testament is *naos*. This word refers to the inner sanctuary as distinct from the whole temple enclosure. *Naos* is used forty-six times in the New Testament. *Naos* comes from a word that means "to inhabit." Therefore, as a noun it refers to the inhabited place. Thus, as far as the Jerusalem Temple was concerned, *naos* was applied to the Holy Place and the Holy of Holies, which composed the inner sanctuary of the Temple. These areas were reserved for the priests alone — no one else could enter. The priests could minister in the Holy Place, but only the high priest could minister in the Holy of Holies — and then only once a year. How sacred the inner sanctuary was to God is indicated by the precise instructions He gave concerning it.

On the basis of the distinction between these two words for "temple," much light is thrown on several passages. In Luke 1 we read that Zacharias went "enter the temple *[naos]* of the Lord" (v. 9) to burn incense and that the people remained "outside" (v. 10). The people were obviously in the Temple area *(hieron)*, but were outside the inner sanctuary *(naos)* where Zacharias was burning incense.

It is also mentioned in the Scriptures that Christ taught in the Temple (Matthew 26:55; Mark 12:35; Luke 19:47). The word used for"temple" in these verses is *hieron,* not *naos,* which would be the inner sanctuary. During His lifetime on earth, Christ was never permitted into the *naos,* or inner sanctuary, for only those who were priests were permitted there. The priests were of the tribe of Levi, but Christ was born of the tribe of Judah and thus would have been excluded from the inner sanctuary of the Temple. This gives us a further glimpse into Christ's humility, as portrayed in Philippians 2. The Lord Jesus Christ was willing not only to give up the outward manifestation of His attributes but also to be born into a tribe that would exclude Him from the inner sanctuary of the Temple, which was inhabited by God. He was willing to be excluded from the special presence of God on earth.

Distinguishing between the two words for "temple" also helps one to have further insights into the hopelessness and disdain for spiritual things that Judas had. Judas covenanted with the chief priests to deliver Jesus to them for thirty pieces of silver. After Jesus had been betrayed and turned over to Pontius Pilate, Judas "felt remorse and returned the thirty pieces of silver to the chief priests and elders, saying, 'I have sinned by betraying innocent blood.' But they said, 'What is that to us? See to that yourself!' And he threw the pieces of silver into the sanctuary *[naos]* and departed; and he went away and hanged himself" (Matthew 27:3-5). Judas threw the thirty pieces of silver into the *naos,* the inner sanctuary, where only the priests were allowed to enter. Not only does this point out Judas's disregard for holy things, it also reveals his utter contempt for the priests to whom he betrayed Christ.

Whereas *hieron* is never used figuratively, *naos* is often used this way. *Naos,* the inner sanctuary, or inhabited place, is used five times in referring to Christ's body. All five of these references have to do with Christ's statement "Destroy this temple *[naos],* and in three days I will raise it up" (John 2:19). The Scriptures are clear, however, that Christ was referring to the "temple of His body" (v. 21). Christ's body was inhabited by God Himself, and therefore it was a temple in the truest sense of the word.

The word *naos* is also used when referring to Christians during the present age (1 Corinthians 3:16-17; 6:19; 2 Corinthians 6:16). First Corinthians 6:19-20 contains the central thought "Or do you not know that your body is a temple of the Holy Spirit who is in you, whom you have from God, and that you are not your own? For you have been bought with a price: therefore glorify God in your body."

Because the Holy Spirit indwells every Christian, the Christian's body is aptly referred to as the *naos,* or inner sanctuary. When we become fully conscious of this truth, it affects our associations (v. 16*a*) and also our care of the body (vv. 16*b*-17).

As we consider how the Jewish mind looked upon the Temple at Jerusalem, it helps us to see how we should consider our own bodies. The Christian's body is the present-day Holy of Holies, for God Himself indwells it.

8

Form: Inner or Outer?

Much theological significance about the Person of Christ hinges on the proper distinction between two words in the Greek New Testament. These words are *morphē* and *schēma*. *Morphē* appears three times in the New Testament (Mark 16:12; Philippians 2:6, 7). *Schēma* occurs twice (1 Corinthians 7:31; Philippians 2:8). It is interesting that three of the five uses of these words occur in three consecutive verses in Philippians 2 that describe the Person of Christ.

Philippians 2 is perhaps one of the most doctrinally significant passages in the entire New Testament, and yet the apostle Paul did not intend it for doctrine as such. Rather, he meant it to be an illustration of the humility of Christ so the believers in Philippi could pattern their lives after Christ. In contrast to haughtiness and selfishness, the apostle said, "Have this attitude in yourselves which was also in Christ Jesus" (v. 5). Then Paul told what Christ did and thereby showed His attitude of mind. The crux of Paul's argument is that if Christ was willing to humble Himself, then Christians should also evidence humility in their lives.

Continuing with his thoughts about Jesus Christ, Paul said, "Who, although He existed in the form of God, did not regard equality with God a thing to be grasped" (v. 6). The word translated "form" in this verse is the word *morphē*. This word emphasizes a permanent, inner form that exists as long as the person exists. Since Christ is eternal, we know that He will always exist. Since He will always exist, He will always be in the "form of God." This verse proves that Christ has a divine nature; therefore, He is God.

Even though Christ, as to His very essence, is God, He "did not regard equality with God a thing to be grasped." Even though Christ was God Himself, He was willing to give up the outward manifestation of the attributes of God in order to come to earth to be the Savior of the world. He did not give up being in the form of God, but He gave up His "equality" with God, as far as the manifestation of His attributes was concerned.

Philippians 2:7 sets forth the contrast: "But emptied Himself, taking the form of a bond-servant, and being made in the likeness of men." Here we have the miracle of miracles — Christ, whose nature is God, took upon Himself the nature of man, thereby becoming the God-Man.

Then we are told in Philippians 2:8, "And being found in appearance as a man, He humbled Himself by becoming obedient to the point of death, even death on a cross." The word translated "appearance" in this verse is *schēma*. This word emphasizes the outward appearance. As to His inner essence, Christ was the God-Man, but outwardly He appeared "as a man."

Some have departed from the teaching of the Scriptures to conclude that since His outward appearance was that of a man, then His inner essence or nature must also have been only that of a man. But the Scriptures make clear that as to His *morphē*, or inner form, Christ was completely God and that at the incarnation He became the God-Man. The Scriptures also clearly show that His humanity was entirely apart from the sin nature of man.

As we consider this passage of Scripture, we become overwhelmed with the thought that One who is God Himself gave up the privileges of manifesting His attributes so He could come to earth and take upon Himself the form of man to die on the cross for our sin.

9
Submission

There has been much discussion about the reference in Scripture stating that wives are to be "submissive" to their husbands (1 Peter 3:1). Some have interpreted this verse to mean that wives are inferior in intellect and ability to their husbands. Others have used these words to show that husbands are to have complete control of every detail involving their wives. In order to gain a proper understanding of the verse, it is necessary to determine the true meaning of the word that is translated "submissive."

The Greek word translated "submissive" in 1 Peter 3:1 is *hupotassō*. The verse says, "In the same way, you wives, be submissive to your own husbands so that even if any of them are disobedient to the word, they may be won without a word by the behavior of their wives." The word *hupotassō* is also translated "submissive" in verse 5: "For in this way in former times the holy women also, who hoped in God, used to adorn themselves, being submissive to their own husbands."

The word *hupotassō* is formed from two Greek words: *hupo*, meaning "under," and *tassō*, meaning "to arrange." *Hupotassō* thus refers to an arrangement of one thing under another.

In biblical times *hupotassō* was used most often as a military term, in the sense of "to rank under." A soldier who ranked under a superior officer would, in this sense, be in subjection to him. This did not necessarily mean that the lower-ranking soldier was inferior in his capabilities or capacities, but it did mean that as far as the line of authority was concerned, he was to be in subjection to his superior officer.

In checking other references where this same word is used, we see other fine shades of meaning. In Luke 10:17 we are told, "And the seventy returned with joy, saying, 'Lord, even the demons are subject to us in Your name.' " *Hupotassō* is translated "subject" in this verse. It is clear that the seventy had superior power and authority over the demons, because they were able to cast out the evil spirits.

The subject of 1 Corinthians 14:32 is the proper exercise of spiritual gifts. Paul was instructing the Corinthians regarding the proper limitations in using their gifts in meetings. For those who might say that they did not have any control over their gifts, Paul said, "And the spirits of prophets are subject to prophets." In this passage, *hupotassō* is also translated "subject." It is apparent here that Paul was telling the believers that Christians are to be in control of the use of their gifts.

In Luke 2 the word *hupotassō* emphasizes the relationship Christ had with His earthly parents: "And He went down with them, and came to Nazareth; and He continued in subjection to them; and His mother treasured all these things in her heart" (v. 51). In His earthly family relationship, Jesus ranked under His parents; therefore, He was subject to them. In addition to other things emphasized in *hupotassō*, the word suggests obedience in this passage. The same emphasis is found in 1 Peter 2:18, where servants are commanded to be subject to their masters.

On instructing women about their part in local church services, especially regarding the gift of speaking in tongues, the apostle Paul wrote: "Let the women keep silent in the churches; for they are not permitted to speak, but let them subject themselves, just as the Law also says" (1 Corinthians 14:34). Here *hupotassō* is translated "subject." In Titus 2:5 wives are commanded to be obedient to their husbands. Thus, *hupotassō* does emphasize the matter of obedience. This is clear in verse 9 of the same passage, where servants are exhorted to be obedient to their masters.

The word translated "submissive" in 1 Peter 3:1 involves power, authority, control, and obedience. The husband ranks over his wife, not because he is superior in intellect or ability, but because God, in His divine order, has placed man in a higher rank of responsibility. This is evident in 1 Corinthians 11:3: "But I want you to understand that Christ is the head of every man, and the man is the head of a woman, and God is the head of Christ."

In 1 Peter 3:6 Sarah is singled out as an illustration of being in subjection to her husband. As one reads the Old Testament accounts about Sarah and Abraham, it is obvious that Abraham required Sarah to do some things that were not especially desirable. But the Scriptures are clear that the one who was responsible before God was the husband. Because Abraham ranked over Sarah in responsibility, God held him responsible for her.

Many objections raised regarding this subjection commonly relate to situations where an unsaved husband requires his Christian wife to do things that violate her spiritual principles. We must remember that such a marriage is not the norm that God intends. The Scriptures are clear that believers should not be yoked with unbelievers (2 Corinthians 6:14). If both the husband and wife were Christians with an equal desire to please Christ in daily living, no doubt a very high percentage of the objections would be solved.

However, it is possible that both persons may have been unsaved at the time of marriage and that the wife became a Christian later. The question then arises as to what the wife should do. The purpose of 1 Peter 3 is to give the Christian wife instruction on how to win her husband to the Lord by being sweet and obedient. Because the husband will not obey the Word, he must be won by the tolerant reasonableness of his wife.

Paul commanded, "Husbands, love your wives, just as Christ also loved the church and gave Himself up for her" (Ephesians 5:25). When husbands obey this command, it becomes a joy for their wives to be in subjection to them.

10

God's Wrath

The wrath of God is not a popular subject today. Theological liberals have explained away the truths of the Scriptures so the popular belief today is that God is a God of love only, not also of wrath. They teach that eventually everyone will be saved from condemnation, because God would not exercise wrath on anyone. The teaching of the Scriptures about the lake of fire is rejected because, they feel, it is unreasonable that there would be a place where men would suffer throughout eternity. Because God is a God of love, no one will suffer wrath from Him.

However, when one reads the Scriptures, he is brought face to face with verses that clearly refer to the wrath of God. The book of Revelation in particular emphasizes God's wrath. Before we examine the verses that tell of God's wrath, it will be helpful to know the significance of the Greek words translated "wrath" in the New Testament.

Thumos is used eighteen times in the New Testament. This word emphasizes a turbulent commotion or boiling agitation of the feelings. It is often temporary, for it emphasizes an outburst of wrath.

Orgē is used thirty-six times in the New Testament. This word emphasizes an abiding or settled habit of mind, frequently with the purpose of revenge. In this regard, *orgē* is more permanent than *thumos*. However, *thumos* — the boiling agitation of the feelings — can become *orgē* — a settled or abiding condition of the mind.

Of the eighteen times that *thumos* occurs in the New Testament, ten are in the book of Revelation. Seven of the ten times in Revelation refer to the wrath of God. Five of those times it is translated "wrath" and twice it is translated "fierce." We are told that anyone who worships the beast and receives his mark will "drink of the wine of the wrath *[thumos]* of God" (14:10).

In the same chapter, the apostle John tells of his vision of Armageddon: "And the angel swung his sickle to the earth, and gathered the clusters from the vine of the earth, and threw them into the great wine press of the wrath *[thumos]* of God" (v. 19). Referring to the seven last plagues, or what is more commonly known as the seven vials or bowls, the apostle John says "in them the wrath *[thumos]* of God is finished" (15:1). Verse 7 of this chapter emphasizes the same truth.

In chapter 16 the seven angels are instructed, " 'Go and pour out the seven bowls of the wrath *[thumos]* of God into the earth' " (v. 1). When the seventh bowl of judgment is poured out, we are told, "And the great city was split into three parts, and the cities of the nations fell. And Babylon the great was remembered before God, to give her the cup of the wine of His fierce *[thumos]* wrath *[orgē]*" (16:19).

Referring to the fall of Babylon, Revelation 18:3 says, "For all the nations have drunk of the wine of the passion *[thumos]* of her immorality, and the kings of the earth have committed acts of immorality with her, and the merchants of the earth have become rich by the wealth of her sensuality."

When the Lord Jesus Christ returns to earth after the Tribulation, it is said of Him that "from His mouth comes a sharp sword, so that with it He may smite the nations; and He will rule them with a rod of iron; and He treads the wine press of the fierce *[thumos]* wrath of *[orgē]* God, the Almighty" (19:15).

Thus we see that *thumos* occurs seven times in the book of Revelation in referring to the wrath of God. Although *thumos* emphasizes an outburst of anger, it is obvious that this is only true from man's viewpoint. For centuries God has been holding back His wrath against sin, but during the Tribulation He will hold it back no longer and will pour it out on the earth.

Orgē, which emphasizes a settled or abiding condition of mind, occurs six times in the book of Revelation, referring only to God's wrath. It occurs in 6:16-17, where we read of those during the Tribulation who say "to the mountains and to the rocks, 'Fall on us and hide us from the presence of Him who sits on the throne, and from the wrath *[orgē]* of the Lamb; for the great day of their wrath *[orgē]* has come; and who is able to stand?' "

When the seventh trumpet is sounded during the Tribulation, we are told that " 'the nations were enraged, and Thy wrath *[orgē]* came' " (11:18). The preceding verse shows clearly that God is the Person referred to. *Orgē* is translated "anger" when describing the doom of the beast-worshipers during the Tribulation: "He also will drink of the wine of the wrath *[thumos]* of God, which is mixed in full strength in the cup of His anger *[orgē];* and he will be tormented with fire and brimstone in the presence of the holy angels and in the presence of the Lamb" (14:10).

As previously cited, Revelation 16:19 refers to God when it speaks of the "His fierce *[thumos]* wrath *[orgē]*." Both of these words are also found in 19:15, which speaks of the "fierce *[thumos]* wrath *[orgē]* of God, the Almighty."

Therefore, the Bible clearly indicates that God is a God of wrath as well as a God of love. He will exercise wrath on all who reject His Son as Savior. All unbelievers will someday stand before the great white throne to be judged by God and then to be cast into the lake of fire (Revelation 20:11-15).

As seen from the use of *orgē* in the book of Revelation, God has a settled wrath against sin. God has not only a permanent love for righteousness but also a permanent hatred for sin. The person who rejects Jesus Christ as Savior will be eternally condemned, but whoever receives Christ as Savior "has eternal life, and does not come into judgment, but has passed out of death into life" (John 5:24).

11

The Great Commission

Evangelical Christians have little doubt about their commission to evangelize the world. However, there are differing opinions about just what is involved in "evangelism." Is a person evangelized when he has heard the gospel once? If so, all we have to do is make sure everyone gets a one-time hearing of the gospel and then our responsibility is fulfilled. However, it is apparent that many people who hear the gospel for the first time do not understand it at all. Our words are just so much noise if people do not understand what we are saying. Does this then mean that no person is evangelized until he understands the gospel? If so, much more is involved in evangelizing the world than making sure everyone hears the gospel once.

Before the Lord Jesus Christ ascended to heaven after His resurrection, He spoke these significant words to His disciples: "Go therefore and make disciples of all the nations, baptizing them in the name of the Father and the Son and the Holy Spirit" (Matthew 28:19). On this occasion, when Christ commanded His disciples to "make disciples" of all the nations, He used a word that is found only three other times in the New Testament. The word is *mathēteuō,* which is the verb form of the common word for "disciple." A disciple is a learner. He is a student, in contrast to a teacher.

The verb found in Matthew 28:19 also appears in 27:57: "And when it was evening, there came a rich man from Arimathea, named Joseph, who himself had also become a disciple of Jesus." The phrase "had also become a disciple of Jesus" is literally "who also himself was discipled by Jesus."

In Matthew 13:52 the same Greek word is translated "has become a disciple" when Jesus said, " 'Therefore every scribe who has become a disciple of the kingdom of heaven is like a head of a household, who brings forth out of his treasure things new and old.' "

This word is also found in Acts 14:21, which says, "And after they had preached the gospel to that city and had made many disciples, they returned to Lystra and to Iconium and to Antioch." Here the word is translated "made many disciples." Paul and Barnabas not only preached the gospel, they also discipled, or taught, many.

The preaching aspect of the Great Commission is seen in Mark 16:15: "And He said to them, 'Go into all the world and preach the gospel to all creation.' " But our responsibility is not fulfilled until we have also heeded the words of Christ recorded in Matthew 28:19: "Make disciples of all the nations."

In Matthew 28:19 the words "go," "make disciples," and "baptizing" are all Greek participles. The tenses of Greek participles are precise in pinpointing the time of their action in relation to the main verbal idea. The main verbal idea in Matthew 28:19 is the phrase "make disciples," which is a translation of a form of the Greek word *mathēteuō*. Around this word all else revolves. The Greek tense of the word "go" indicates that the going takes place before the discipling. Obviously, in order to disciple the nations, we have to go to them by some means.

The word "baptizing" is in a Greek tense that indicates the baptizing is to be done during the same time the discipling is taking place. As we are teaching others the Word of God, it is important that we be baptizing those who identify themselves with the Lord Jesus Christ. The idea is not that we disciple one year and baptize the converts the next; rather, the baptizing is to be done while the discipling is being done.

In addition to baptizing while discipling, verse 20 uses another Greek participle, translated "teaching." This is the common word for "teach," and this verse precisely spells out what is to be taught: "Teaching them to observe all that I commanded you."

The responsibility of Christians is to disciple all the nations, thereby making them adherents to the teaching of the Word of God. Evangelism, therefore, is more than just giving a person a one-time hearing of the gospel. Evangelism, in essence, is teaching. It is teaching the unbeliever what God has said about his sin. It is teaching him what Jesus Christ accomplished on the cross when He paid the penalty of sin. It is teaching him how he can become a child of God by placing his faith in Jesus Christ as his Savior. Having discipled a person in these truths, we can consider him evangelized when he is able to make a knowledgeable decision for or against Jesus Christ.

12

A Savior Is Born

The original language helps one to dig below the surface of the
Christmas story in Luke 2 and gain many interesting insights.
When you have discovered some of these treasures, the reading of
Luke 2 becomes an even richer experience.

Luke tells us that Caesar Augustus gave a decree that "a census
be taken of all the inhabited earth" (v. 1). The word translated "inhabited earth" is *oikoumenē*. This word was used originally by the
Greeks to designate the land they possessed in contrast to the land
of the barbarians. When the Greeks later became subject to the
Romans, the word was used in referring to the entire Roman
world. Still later it was used to refer to the inhabited earth. It is
from this word that we get the word "ecumenical." Obviously in
Luke 2:1 it has reference to everyone under the jurisdiction of
Caesar Augustus.

Luke also tells us that Joseph and Mary went to Bethlehem so
they could be registered. It was while they were at Bethlehem that
Mary "gave birth to her first-born son; and she wrapped Him in
clothes, and laid Him in a manger, because there was no room for
them in the inn" (v. 7).

The "clothes" in which Mary wrapped the baby Jesus refers to
swathing bands of cloth, which would be known in modern Eng-

lish simply as "cloth bands." There is insufficient support to main-
tain that these were rags, as some have claimed in emphasizing the
poor conditions in which the Lord Jesus Christ was born.

Luke says, "And in the same region there were some shepherds
staying out in the fields, and keeping watch over their flock by
night" (v. 8). Historically, it is known that a flock was kept in the
vicinity for the purpose of Temple sacrifice. Although we cannot
be sure that these shepherds were watching such a flock, it would
be highly significant to the shepherds involved if the angel an-
nounced to them the birth of the Lamb of God, who came to be
the sacrifice for sin and to put an end to the Temple sacrifices.

The angel who appeared to the shepherds is not named, but his
message was very precise. He told the shepherds, "Do not be
afraid; for behold, I bring you good news of a great joy which
shall be for all the people" (v. 10). The shepherds "were terribly
frightened" (v. 9); literally, they "feared a great fear." The reason
was that the angel bore "good news of a great joy."

The word translated "good news" is *euaggelizomai,* from which
we get our word "evangelize." It was good news that the angel
proclaimed to the shepherds; therefore, they had no reason to
fear. The angel said that the good news of great joy was to be to all
the people. "All the people" specifically refers to the nation of
Israel, because Christ had come to be its Messiah and Savior. It was
then intended that the nation of Israel would proclaim the good
news to everyone that Jesus Christ had come to die for the sins of
the whole world" (1 John 2:2).

The angel emphasized to the shepherds that in the city of David
was born a "Savior, who is Christ the Lord" (Luke 2:11). The angel did not refer to the Lord Jesus Christ as "Teacher" or "Great
Example," nor even as "Messiah," but as "Savior." A savior is one
who brings deliverance, and Christ came to pay the penalty for
the sin of mankind so everyone could be delivered from condemnation by receiving Christ as Savior. That He was also to be the
Messiah of Israel is seen in His name "Christ," which means
"Messiah."

The angel told the shepherds how they would recognize the
Child: "You will find a baby wrapped in cloths, and lying in a
manger" (v. 12). Luke recorded that after this announcement of

the angel, "suddenly there appeared with the angel a multitude of the heavenly host praising God, and saying, 'Glory to God in the highest, and on earth peace among men with whom He is pleased' " (vv. 13-14).

Notice in the verses above that peace is not promised to all people. The NASB translates the Greek words accurately when it says, "peace among men with whom He is pleased" (v. 14). This makes the meaning clear. There is no peace for the person who has rejected God. The Bible emphasizes this when it says, " 'There is no peace,' says my God, 'to the wicked' " (Isaiah 57:21).

The shepherds went to find the newborn Savior, and having found Him, they told others about the Child. Luke commented, "And all that heard it wondered at the things which were told them by the shepherds" (Luke 2:18). In contrast to these who were obviously discussing these matters publicly, Luke said, "But Mary treasured up all these things, pondering them in her heart" (v. 19).

When Luke wrote that Mary "treasured up" all of these things, he used a compound word that emphasized that Mary kept these things "with" or "within" herself. Luke also used a tense that emphasized that Mary continually kept all of these things in her heart.

Luke said Mary was also "pondering" these things. Here we are given an insight into Mary's heart. While others were discussing the significance of the birth of Christ, as a mother she was inwardly reflecting about what she had been told and had experienced regarding the birth of Jesus. Mary surely told her friends about many of these things, but as a mother there were some things that were too tender and precious to share with anyone.

13
Praying Without Ceasing

One of the first things a new Christian usually hears is that all Christians should "pray without ceasing." Although he is slow to admit his problem to older Christians, the new Christian soon realizes that no matter how good a prayer life he has, by no stretch of the imagination could it be said that he prays without ceasing. He knows there are many times during the day when he is not praying; therefore, he feels guilty for not measuring up to the command of the Scriptures.

But what do the Scriptures really mean when they exhort the believer to "pray without ceasing"? The word that is translated "without ceasing" is *adialeiptos*. This adverb appears four times in the New Testament, and all references are associated with prayer. The first occurrence of this word is in Romans 1:9, where the apostle Paul tells the Roman Christians, "For God, whom I serve in my spirit in the preaching of the gospel of His Son, is my witness as to how unceasingly I make mention of you." Here it is the "making mention" that is without ceasing.

The same Greek word appears in 1 Thessalonians 1:3, where Paul assures the Thessalonian Christians, "Constantly bearing in mind your work of faith and labor of love and steadfastness of hope in our Lord Jesus Christ in the presence of our God and Father." Here it is the remembering that is without ceasing, but verse 2 makes clear that the remembering is closely associated with Paul's praying.

The third occurrence of *adialeiptos* is in 1 Thessalonians 2:13, where Paul writes: "And for this reason we also constantly thank God that when you received from us the word of God's message, you accepted it not as the word of men, but for what it really is, the word of God, which also performs its work in you who believe." Here it is the thanking that is without ceasing.

The last occurrence of *adialeiptos* is in the most commonly known reference, 1 Thessalonians 5:17, which records the apostle Paul's command, "Pray without ceasing."

We see then that the adverb *adialeiptos* is used four times in the New Testament — and only by the apostle Paul — and that all four references are associated with prayer. Paul mentions, remembers, thanks, and urges believers to pray "without ceasing."

The adjectival form of this word occurs twice and emphasizes the same meaning. One of these occurrences is in Romans 9:2, where Paul emphasizes the "continual" sorrow in his heart. The other is in 2 Timothy 1:3, where the word is again associated with praying. In this verse the apostle Paul assured Timothy, "I thank God, whom I serve with a clear conscience the way my forefathers did, as I constantly remember you in my prayers night and day." Here the adjectival form of *adialeiptos* is translated "constantly."

Thus we see that whether this Greek word appears as an adverb or as an adjective, five of the six times it is translated "without ceasing."

But the question remains: Is it really possible to pray constantly or without ceasing? The answer is found in discovering that during the Roman period, the word *adialeiptos* was used in describing a cough. No matter how serious a person's cough, it would not be one, long, drawn-out cough but rather, coughing at short intervals. Although at a given moment a person might not be coughing, it would not be said that he had stopped coughing.

The word *adialeiptos* comes from the word *dialeipō*, which means "stop," or "cease." The "a" prefix is the Greek way of making a negative, so that *adialeiptos* means "not stopping," or "not ceasing."

As we relate this information to the matter of praying, we see that the Christian is not expected to be involved in a single, never-ending prayer; rather, he is to pray constantly. ("Constant" implies uniform or persistent occurrence or recurrence.) Although we should always be in a prayerful attitude, it is obvious that we cannot be engaged in one continual prayer. Just as a person with a cough may cough frequently, we should be praying at frequent intervals for those whom God has laid on our hearts.

It should never be said of us that we have stopped praying. Instead, our goal should be to make the intervals shorter, so that less and less time elapses during which we are not communing with the Lord. Throughout each day we should be sharing with Him the things in our hearts. There should be a time each day when we have a concentrated period of prayer, but throughout the day we should be responding to the Lord and praying as we are led by the Holy Spirit.

14
Dead or Alive?

Every spiritual blessing a believer has is the result of what the Lord Jesus Christ accomplished when He died on the cross. Many Christians are not aware of the centrality of the cross in providing not only deliverance from the penalty of sin but also deliverance from its power.

Whereas some Christians have neglected emphasizing what Christ accomplished through His death on the cross, others have almost entirely concentrated their attention on the cross. As a result, many are still living at the cross, which is the place of death. It is important that we know what the Scriptures teach about the significance of Christ's death on the cross, but having seen those truths, we need to go on to further teaching.

The Scriptures emphasize two aspects of salvation. When a person receives Christ as Savior, his sins are forgiven — but this in itself is not sufficient. If this were all that is accomplished by receiving Christ as Savior, it would be like removing the bullet from a dead man's head — the cause of death would be removed, but he still would not have life.

When we receive Christ as Savior, not only are our sins forgiven but also God gives life to us. God imputes His righteousness to the one receiving Christ as Savior. This truth is seen in 2 Corinthians

5:21: "He [God] made Him [Christ] who knew no sin to be sin on our behalf, that we might become the righteousness of God in Him."

There are two important things that happen to the person when he places his faith in Christ. One is that at that very moment he partakes of the benefits of all that Christ accomplished when He was crucified. Therefore, it can be said that the believer actually died with Christ. Romans 6 emphasizes the believer's death with Christ. But there is the additional matter of the believer's being made alive. We should understand and appreciate what was accomplished by our death with Christ, but we must not stop there. We must see the importance of living, which results from our being resurrected with Christ. Romans 6 also emphasizes this truth.

These fundamental truths are seen in the fine shades of meaning in the Greek tenses. Romans 6:11 is a key verse on this subject. In this verse the apostle Paul writes: "Even so consider yourselves to be dead to sin, but alive to God in Christ Jesus."

The adjectives "dead" and "alive" are used as if two states of existence are all that is being emphasized. Although this is not inaccurate, there is more that is emphasized in the Greek tenses. The word that is translated "dead" emphasizes an event that has already taken place. Each individual was potentially co-crucified with Christ on the cross. When he receives Christ as his Savior, the believer receives the benefits of the cross so his state of existence is that he is dead to sin. However, the word translated "alive" is not an adjective but rather a participle whose tense emphasizes continuous action in the present time. Thus, although the believer is said to be dead to sin, he is to be living unto God. To say that a person is "alive" may mean that he is just existing. But to emphasize that he is to be living *unto God* indicates an abundant life that does not show up in the word "alive."

Galatians 2:20 brings out much the same truth as Romans 6:11. In the Galatians passage the apostle Paul writes: "I have been crucified with Christ; and it is no longer I who live, but Christ lives in me; and the life which I now live in the flesh I live by faith in the Son of God, who loved me, and delivered Himself up for me." The word translated "crucified" is in the perfect tense in the

Greek. This tense emphasizes that the act had been completed in the past and that its effect continues. The believer's crucifixion is a completed act of the past. It is not something that is presently going on.

However, in contrast to the crucifixion, which was completed in the past with a continuing effect, Paul says, "It is no longer I who live." The word translated "live" is in the present tense, as is the word translated "alive" in Romans 6:11. So also in Galatians 2:20 the apostle Paul is emphasizing the living aspect of Christianity. He is not simply dwelling on what has taken place in the past; rather, he is emphasizing the abundant life that every Christian should have. Paul became a partaker of the benefits of the crucifixion of Christ through faith, and his vibrant living for the Lord was also based on faith. Paul said, "The life which I now live in the flesh I live by faith in the Son of God." The reason Paul had such an abundant life was that Christ was living in him and Paul was living by the faithfulness, or steadfastness, of Christ.

Not enough of us are "present-tense Christians." Most of us seem to be living in the past inasmuch as we are constantly looking back to what has been accomplished for us in the past. Our crucifixion with Christ is essential to spiritual life, but we must also emphasize the present tense of living for Him. We live for Him by making our lives available to His control so He can effectively live out His life through us.

Sometimes one hears a Christian telling another that every day he is to crucify himself anew in order to properly live for Christ. Such teaching does not find support in the Scriptures because the Christian's crucifixion is something that has been completed in the past and will never be repeated. In supporting their crucifying-of-self teaching, many refer to Paul's statement in 1 Corinthians 15:31, where he says, "I die daily." However, the context does not bear out that Paul is talking about crucifying himself daily. In verse 30 Paul asks, "Why are we also in danger every hour?" He is referring to the fact that he constantly lives in the presence of physical danger and possible death. This is supported by verse 32, where he says, "If from human motives I fought with wild beasts at Ephesus, what does it profit me? If the dead are not raised, let us eat and drink, for tomorrow we die." The surrounding verses indicate that verse 31 refers to Paul's constantly living in the danger of physical death.

The Christian's need is not to crucify himself but rather to appropriate what Christ accomplished through His death on the cross. This is what Paul refers to in Romans 6:11, where he exhorts the Roman Christians to consider themselves to be dead to sin but living unto God. They were to count as a fact their crucifixion with Christ and then go on to live for Him. We do not become spiritual by doing things for Christ; we become spiritual by appropriating what Christ has done for us.

15
Testing: For Good or Evil?

James wrote: "Consider it all joy, my brethren, when you encounter various trials" (James 1:2). In verse 12 of this same chapter, he writes: "Blessed is a man who perseveres under trial; for once he has been approved, he will receive the crown of life, which the Lord has promised to those who love Him." However, a problem arises when the next verse is read, because it says, "Let no one say when he is tempted, 'I am being tempted by God'; for God cannot be tempted by evil, and He Himself does not tempt anyone." On the one hand it seems that temptations are sent to us from God, and we are to consider it a privilege to pass through them, but on the other hand we are told that God does not tempt any man.

In order to understand these verses, it is necessary to know the meaning of the words that are translated by forms of "trial" and "tempt." The same Greek word is used in all three of the verses just quoted from James, yet there are obviously different shades of meaning intended. The word is used in its noun form in verses 2 and 12 and in its verb form in verse 13. The noun is *peirasmos,* and the verb is *peirazō.* The root word of these forms has such meanings as "test," "try," "prove." The matter of significance about *peirazō* is that it is used in both a good sense and a bad sense.

It can have the idea of testing with the purpose of bringing out that which is good, or it can have the idea of testing with the purpose of bringing out that which is bad.

When the word is used in regard to Satan, it has the bad sense of bringing out that which is evil or soliciting to evil. Satan himself is known as "the tempter" (Matthew 4:3). Satan thought he could get Christ to respond to evil, but because Christ is God, there was nothing in Him that responded to evil. Christ told Satan, " 'You shall not put the Lord your God to the test' " (4:7). Satan was not trying to bring out that which was good in Jesus but was endeavoring to solicit Him to evil.

When Ananias and Sapphira lied about the amount they had received for their land, Peter asked Sapphira, "Why is it that you have agreed together to put the Spirit of the Lord to the test?" (Acts 5:9). They were not trying to bring out that which was good in the Lord, so the word is used in its bad sense in this context.

The word *peirazō* is used in 2 Corinthians 13:5, where Paul tells the Corinthians, "Test yourselves to see if you are in the faith." In this context the Corinthians were obviously to look at the good as well as the bad in their lives. So the word is also used in a good sense. Thus, in the book of James, the "various trials" have a good purpose in view — to bring out that which is good in the believers. This is why they should "count it all joy." This is also true regarding James 1:12. However, the word is used in its negative sense in verse 13, as is evident from the words "God cannot be tempted by evil." In the phrase "and He Himself does not tempt anyone," the words "with evil" are to be understood. Therefore, God never solicits a person to do evil; rather, He brings tests into a person's life that will bring out that which is good in him.

First Corinthians 10:13 uses both *peirasmos* and *peirazō* in their good sense: "No temptation has overtaken you but such as is common to man; and God is faithful, who will not allow you to be tempted beyond what you are able, but with the temptation will provide the way of escape also, that you may be able to endure it." God sends tests and trials into our lives to bring out that which is good in us, and He always provides the strength necessary to bear up under the tests.

Another Greek word was frequently used when the writer wanted to emphasize a testing with the purpose of bringing out that which is good. This word is *dokimazō*. Whereas *peirazō* could be used in either a good or bad sense, *dokimazō* is used only in the good sense. In this regard it has to do with proving in order to approve.

One such occurrence is Romans 12:2: "And do not be conformed to this world, but be transformed by the renewing of your mind, that you may prove what the will of God is, that which is good and acceptable and perfect."

Dokimazō is translated "try them out" in Luke 14:19: "And another one said, 'I have bought five yoke of oxen, and I am going to try them out; please consider me excused.' " The excuse this person used for not attending the great supper was that he wanted to try out his yoke of oxen to see how good they were.

In 1 Corinthians 3, which tells of the judgment seat of Christ, *dokimazō* is translated "will test" in verse 13: "Each man's work will become evident; for the day will show it, because it is to be revealed with fire; and the fire itself will test the quality of each man's work." This helps us to see that at the judgment seat of Christ the emphasis will be on discovering that which is good so that it might be rewarded. Only those who have received Jesus Christ as Savior will appear before the judgment seat of Christ. The purpose of the judgment will be not to condemn but to reward that which is good. The believer has been delivered from all condemnation through faith in Christ.

The understanding of this Greek word also helps us to see what God's purpose is in sending trials of our faith. First Peter 1:7 says, "That the proof of your faith, being more precious than gold which is perishable, even though tested by fire, may be found to result in praise and glory and honor at the revelation of Jesus Christ." The word "tested" is a noun form of *dokimazō*. Thus we see that the purpose for the trials of our faith is that God might bring out that which is good and that we might become mature Christians.

Because *peirazō* has both good and bad meanings, it can be used in regard to both God and Satan. However, *dokimazō* can never be used for Satan because he never tests to prove that which is good but rather to solicit to evil.

16

A Decision or a Feeling?

What must a person do to come into a right relationship with Jesus Christ? When asked this question, a person acquainted with the Scriptures may quote such a verse as Luke 13:3, which records the words of Christ, who said, " 'I tell you, no, but, unless you repent, you will all likewise perish.' " A problem arises, however, in determining what is included in the word "repent." The word is commonly used today as meaning only "to be sorry for." It is important to understand the true meaning of the word "repent," because those who do not repent will perish.

The word translated "repent" in Luke 13:3 is *metanoeō*. This word means much more than just being sorry for past actions; it emphasizes a change of mind.

When John the Baptist appeared in the wilderness of Judea, his message was, "Repent, for the kingdom of heaven is at hand" (Matthew 3:2). Because Jesus would soon appear as the Messiah, John wanted the people to be spiritually ready for His coming. John the Baptist was not asking the people just to be sorry for their sins; he wanted them to change their minds about Jesus Christ. Those who did not realize their spiritual need for a right relationship with the Messiah obviously needed to change their minds about their spiritual condition and about the Person of the Messiah.

When Jesus Christ appeared, He was rejected as the Messiah and was crucified for claiming to be the Son of God. Because He was God in the flesh, man could not have crucified Him without His being willing. John 19:10-11 tells us, "Pilate therefore said to Him, 'You do not speak to me? Do You not know that I have authority to release You, and I have authority to crucify You?' Jesus answered, 'You would have no authority over Me, unless it had been given you from above; for this reason he who delivered Me up to you has the greater sin.' "

When Jesus died on the cross, His death satisfied God the Father for the sins of the world. The apostle John wrote of Christ: "And He Himself is the propitiation for our sins; and not for ours only, but also for those of the whole world" (1 John 2:2). The question that remains is, How can Christ's payment for sin be applied to an individual? It is not applied just because a person is sorry for his sin. He may be sorry only because he has been caught in his sin, or he may be genuinely sorry because of the consequences of sinning. In either case, being sorry for his sin does not bring a person into right relationship with Jesus Christ.

What is needed in addition is made clear in John 1:11-12: "He came to His own, and those who were his own did not receive Him. But as many as received Him, to them He gave the right to become children of God, even to those who believe in His name." It is necessary for a person to receive Jesus Christ as his Savior in order to become a child of God. For a person to receive Christ as the One who has paid the penalty for his sin, he must change his mind about his sin and about Christ as the Savior. It takes an act of the will to receive Christ as Savior. It is a choice that results from changing the mind about sin and about the Savior. To those who make this decision, Christ Himself has promised, "He who hears My word, and believes Him who sent Me, has eternal life, and does not come into judgment, but has passed out of death into life" (John 5:24).

Those who make the decision to receive Christ as Savior doubtlessly have sorrow over the sins of the past and the wasted years of living for self. But it was not the sorrow that changed their eternal destiny; only the change of mind that resulted in the decision to receive Christ as Savior was able to change their eternal destiny.

There is a word in the Greek New Testament that emphasizes sorrow and regret. This is *metamelomai*. This word is used in Matthew 27:3: "Then when Judas, who had betrayed Him, saw that He had been condemned, he felt remorse and returned the thirty pieces of silver to the chief priests and elders." Judas sorrowed because He was condemned and even confessed his sin to the chief priests and elders: " 'I have sinned by betraying innocent blood.' But they said, 'What is that to us? See to that yourself!' And he threw the pieces of silver into the sanctuary and departed; and he went away and hanged himself" (vv. 4-5). Judas was sorry because of his sin, but he did not have a change of mind about his sin and about Jesus Christ that resulted in his receiving Christ as Savior. From the life of Judas it is evident that being sorry for sin is not enough.

If you have never made the decision to receive Christ as Savior, remember from the experience of Judas that just being sorry for your sin will not enable you to escape eternal condemnation. Turn to Jesus Christ and receive Him as Savior today. When you receive Him into your life, He will forgive you of your sin, deliver you from all condemnation, and give you eternal life.

17

Perfect: Sinless Perfection or Spiritual Maturity?

The word "perfect," as it appears in various translations, has caused some Bible students to draw the conclusion that it is possible for believers to live above all sin. Such a teaching is sometimes referred to as "sinless perfection." It teaches that believers are able to reach a point in life where they no longer commit sin. Some even talk of the old nature as being "eradicated," which enables the believer to live without ever sinning.

The word translated "perfect" in some translations is *teleios*. Its verb form is *teleioō*. The shades of meaning involved in these words reveal that something quite different from sinless perfection is intended by their use. In particular, these words emphasize that which is full-grown, or mature. Thus they often emphasize the finished product, whether it be maturity in a person or the finishing of a work.

The apostle Paul wrote to the Corinthians: "Brethren, do not be children in your thinking; yet in evil be babes, but in your thinking be mature" (1 Corinthians 14:20). The word translated "mature" in this verse is the noun *teleios*. It is evident in this verse that the apostle Paul was drawing a contrast between children and

adults. Paul was not encouraging the Corinthians to strive for sinless perfection but to evidence understanding that would be expected of mature adults.

A form of the same Greek word is found in Hebrews 5:14: "But
solid food is for the mature, who because of practice have their
senses trained to discern good and evil." Here the word is translated "mature." This verse indicates that in order for us to become
spiritually mature, we must exercise our senses in discerning both
good and evil. We become mature as we make it a practice to apply the Word of God to daily situations.

James told his readers, "Knowing that the testing of your faith
produces endurance" (James 1:3). Then he said, "And let endurance have its perfect result, that you may be perfect and complete,
lacking in nothing" (v. 4). Both of the words translated "perfect"
in verse 4 are forms of *teleios.* James was emphasizing the end product of patience. The testing of faith works patience, which results
in a mature, well-rounded Christian.

There will be a day when all Christians will be sinlessly perfect — when they leave this life and go to be with Christ. But concerning this life, the apostle John wrote: "If we say that we have
no sin, we are deceiving ourselves, and the truth is not in us. If we
confess our sins, He is faithful and righteous to forgive us our sins
and to cleanse us from all unrighteousness. If we say that we have
not sinned, we make Him a liar, and His word is not in us" (1 John
1:8-10).

The Christian today can only be "perfect" in the sense that he is
to be a mature individual who honors the Lord in his daily living.
Such a Christian walks in accordance with the standards of his
holy God. (See chapter 3 for further discussion on sinless
perfection.)

18
Restoring a Spiritual Brother

The apostle Paul exhorted all believers when he said, "Brethren, even if a man is caught in any trespass, you who are spiritual, restore such a one in a spirit of gentleness; each one looking to yourself, lest you too be tempted" (Galatians 6:1).

It is one thing to recognize the need of restoring a brother who has committed an act of sin, but it is quite another thing to rightly handle the situation. Most believers would want to avoid confronting such a person with his sin because of the reaction that might result. However, Paul presented the matter as an imperative for those who are "spiritual."

Those who qualify as spiritual Christians are those who live according to what Paul wrote in the previous chapter of Galatians. Paul instructed believers, "Walk by the Spirit, and you will not carry out the desire of the flesh" (5:16). The characteristics of the spiritual person are known as "the fruit of the Spirit," listed in verses 22 and 23: "Love, joy, peace, patience, kindness, goodness, faithfulness, gentleness, self-control; against such things there is no law." In verse 25 the apostle exhorts, "If we live by the Spirit, let us also walk by the Spirit." It is the person who lives in accordance with these principles that Paul referred to as "spiritual."

Those who are spiritual are to "restore" the person overtaken in a fault. The word translated "restore" is *katartizō*. In order for us to know all that is involved in restoring a fallen believer, we need to know the shades of meaning involved in the word Paul used for "restore."

In tracing this word in its secular and biblical uses, one finds that it was used for reconciling factions. Certainly that is involved in Galatians 6:1. A brother needs to be reconciled. The word was also used in referring to the setting of bones. From such a use we can see that restoration often involves suffering. It would also indicate that the one doing the restoring must be knowledgeable about what he is doing. He would not want to cause unnecessary pain, but he would realize that proper treatment often involves pain.

In Mark 1:19, a form of this same Greek word is translated "mending" when it says that Christ "saw James the son of Zebedee, and John his brother, who were also in the boat mending the nets." Some commentators believe that the word refers to a "folding" of the nets rather than a "mending" of them, but in either case the nets were being prepared for further use. So also the spiritual believer is to restore a fallen brother so he might be useful to the Lord.

When Paul used the word translated "restore," he put it in a tense that emphasizes continuous action. In choosing this tense, the apostle Paul was stressing that such restoration involves a process, not just a single act. Those who have been used of the Lord to restore fallen brothers to a place of usefulness know the degree of patience and perseverance that is needed.

The apostle Paul instructed that such restoration must be done "in the spirit of meekness." This is one of the characteristics Paul listed under the fruit of the Spirit, recorded in the previous chapter. The word "meekness" is a rich study in itself. Its chief characteristic seems to be that it combines strength and gentleness. The spiritual believer is one who is mature and strong in the things of the Lord and who has great compassion for those who are weak — those "caught in any trespass." Meekness is the opposite of pride and is often used in contrast to pride. This is true even in the context in Galatians. In the last verse of chapter 5 Paul says, "Let us not become boastful, challenging one another, envying one another." In contrast to being like this, Paul said that we should restore fallen brothers in the spirit of gentleness.

Paul also reminded his readers, "Looking to yourself, lest you too be tempted" (6:1). When we realize that none of us is immune to temptations, it will cause us to be more gentle and sympathetic with others who have yielded to temptation. Every believer should realize that because he still has the old nature, he is capable of falling into sin. Such a realization greatly changes our attitude toward those who have fallen.

19
Negative Commands

There are many negative commands given in the New Testament. When a person or group is commanded not to do something, the context usually indicates whether they were or were not doing it at the time the command was given. Several Greek grammars show the Greek language had a way of indicating in its construction whether or not the action was going on at the time of the command. More recent research, however, finds it is safer to rely on the context than on any particular construction in Greek to indicate when the action was taking place. This is not an unusual characteristic of New Testament Greek. Most languages depend heavily on context to determine shades of meaning. So the better we are acquainted with the context, the better interpreters of God's Word we will be — whether we have a knowledge of Greek or not.

If the action was *not* going on, the negative command could be given to forbid the action from ever beginning. To indicate this kind of prohibition, the aorist tense was normally used in the negative command. However, the context must be the final authority in determining whether or not the action was already in progress. Such is the case in Luke 11:4, where Christ instructed His disciples to pray, "Lead us not into temptation." Because God tempts no man with evil (see James 1:13 and the discussion of this topic in chapter 15 of this book), it is apparent in Luke 11:4 that the action had not been going on. It is as if the person praying were saying, "Don't even begin to lead us into temptation."

When Jesus was crucified, the soldiers divided up His garments. But of His coat they said, "Let us not tear it, but cast lots for it" (John 19:24). It was not that they were rending, or tearing, it and decided to stop; rather, they had not begun to tear it. This is indicated by the context, so one could translate this negative prohibition: "Don't begin to tear it."

When the action *was* going on and a command was given for it to stop, the present tense was normally used in the negative command, but again the context must indicate whether action was or was not in progress. When Jesus found the money changers in the Temple and those who were selling oxen, sheep, and doves, He drove them out of the Temple and commanded them: "Stop making My Father's house a house of merchandise" (John 2:16). The context makes clear that they were already making His Father's house a house of merchandise. This is why the NASB translates the command as "Stop making."

Concerning whether action was already in progress or not, notice Acts 18:9: "And the Lord said to Paul in the night by a vision, 'Do not be afraid any longer, but go on speaking and do not be silent.'" The question arises, Was the Lord telling Paul not to even begin being afraid or to stop being afraid? There are those who say Paul had no fear as he went everywhere preaching the gospel. The construction of Acts 18:9 uses the present tense in the negative command. However, this might only mean the Lord was commanding Paul not to be fearing from this point onward. But what do the Scriptures indicate? Did Paul experience fear as he went everywhere proclaiming the gospel?

It is true that the apostle Paul was not ashamed of the gospel, for he wrote: "For I am not ashamed of the gospel, for it is the power of God for salvation to everyone who believes, to the Jew first and also to the Greek" (Romans 1:16). Although he had no reservations about the power of the gospel, this did not mean he was free of all fear in presenting the gospel. In 1 Corinthians 2:3, the apostle reminds the Corinthians, "I was with you in weakness and in fear and in much trembling." It is understandable that Paul would have had concern and fear as he came to the city of Corinth, which had a population of over half a million and which was full of perverted sex and wickedness of every kind. However, he had no reservations about the ability of the gospel to change lives if people would put it to the test.

Thus, in Acts 18:9 the Lord is probably commanding Paul to stop fearing and to speak. Verse 10 tells of the assurance the Lord gave Paul: " 'For I am with you, and no man will attack you in order to harm you, for I have many people in this city.' "

20

A Condition or an Assumption?

As in English, the New Testament Greek commonly uses an "if" to introduce a condition. There are three main kinds of conditional sentences in Greek. One is that of simple condition: "If you study, you will learn." The conclusion in this conditional sentence is no more sure than the condition — if one does not study, he will not learn. If it can be determined that the person is studying, this conditional sentence can be translated: "Since you are studying, you will learn."

Another conditional sentence is contrary-to-fact: "If you would have studied, you would have learned." Inasmuch as the person did not study, he did not learn.

There is also a condition of uncertainty: "If you study, you will learn." Notice that this example is the same as that of the simple condition. However, this one indicates it is uncertain whether or not one will study. In English, one would have to distinguish between these two examples by context alone, but in Greek there are distinct constructions that clearly indicate which condition is intended.

In English the word *if* is commonly used to introduce a condi-

tion — "If you pay for this item, you may have it for your own."
However, the word *if* is also used in the English language to indicate something that is assumed true — "If you are the owner of
the house, you are responsible to keep it in good repair."

These uses of the word *if* were also common in New Testament
Greek. Whereas in English we have to rely almost entirely on context to determine the use that is intended, the writers of the New
Testament used different grammatical constructions to indicate
what use they intended. Perhaps the most unusual use to the English reader is that where the condition is assumed to be true.

In Mark 4:23, it is evident by the context that the condition is assumed true: "If any man has ears to hear, let him hear." Because
man does have ears to hear, he should hear and heed.

Colossians contains three verses where the word *if* does not introduce a condition to be met but rather something that Paul assumed true about the Colossians. Paul wrote: "And although you
were formerly alienated and hostile in mind, engaged in evil
deeds, yet He has now reconciled you in His fleshly body through
death, in order to present you before Him holy and blameless and
beyond reproach — if indeed you continue in the faith firmly es-
tablished and steadfast, and not moved away from the hope of the
gospel that you have heard, which was proclaimed in all creation
under heaven, and of which I, Paul, was made a minister (1:21-
23). In the phrase "if indeed you continue in the faith firmly es-
tablished and steadfast," *if* could be translated "since," or "because." Paul was not presenting a condition to be met; he was
stating something true about the Colossians. Because the Colossians had been reconciled to God by their decision to receive
Christ as Savior, they could count on the fact that they would be
presented holy, unblamable, and unreprovable in His sight.

Concerning the Colossians, Paul also said, "If you have died
with Christ to the elementary principles of the world, why, as if
you were living in the world, do you submit yourself to decrees"
(2:20). Again the word "if" is used with the meaning "since," or
"because." Paul knew that these people had received Jesus Christ
as their Savior and had died with Him, and in the light of that, he
was asking why they continued living in subjection to human
ordinances.

Paul also reminded the Colossian Christians, "If then you have been raised up with Christ, keep seeking the things above, where Christ is, seated at the right hand of God" (3:1). From the context we see Paul was assuming that the Colossians had the right relationship with Christ, and because of this he was exhorting them to keep seeking those things that are above. Because of their position with Christ he urged them: "Set your mind on the things above, not on the things that are on earth" (v. 2).

It is impossible to merit position with God. The way of salvation is the same for each person — by grace through faith. Even as salvation is not *ob*tained through works, neither is it *re*tained through works. Each person's salvation is completely dependent on the sufficiency of Christ's death by which He paid the penalty for sins. However, having received eternal life through faith in Jesus Christ, there are a multitude of things the Christian can do to express this relationship to others. Good works are the result of a right relationship with Jesus Christ but never the means of attaining this relationship.

21

Indifferent Following or Intense Pursuit?

In giving inspired counsel to a young pastor by the name of Timothy, the apostle Paul said, "Now flee from youthful lusts, and pursue righteousness, faith, love and peace, with those who call on the Lord from a pure heart" (2 Timothy 2:22). Paul's counsel involved a twofold responsibility: fleeing and following. The apostle Paul did not subscribe to the philosophy that a person becomes a stronger Christian by purposely submitting himself to temptation so he might become stronger through resisting it. The clear command to Timothy was, "Flee from youthful lusts."

Paul knew that Timothy could not become spiritually mature just by avoiding certain things; therefore, he commanded him to pursue that which was really important. Fleeing is the negative aspect; following, or pursuing, is the positive.

The word the apostle Paul used for "pursue" left no doubt as to the efforts Timothy would have to put forth if he were to successfully follow these things. In commanding Timothy to pursue righteousness, Paul uses the word *diōkō*. Of the forty-four times this word appears in the Greek New Testament, thirty-one references have to do with persecution. Christ used forms of this word in the Beatitudes when He said, " 'Blessed are those which have been persecuted *[diōkō]* for the sake of righteousness, for theirs is the kingdom of heaven. Blessed are you when men cast insults at you, and persecute *[diōkō]* you, and say all kinds of evil against you falsely, on account of Me. Rejoice, and be glad, for your reward in heaven is great, for so they persecuted *[diōkō]* the prophets who were before you" (Matthew 5:10-12). Paul used *diōkō* in the sense of persecution when he said, "For you have heard of my former manner of life in Judaism, how I used to persecute *[diōkō]* the church of God beyond measure, and tried to destroy it" (Galatians 1:13).

At first it might seem strange that one word could have two such different meanings — "persecution" as well as "pursue." The word *diōkō* has the meaning of "to run after, pursue, strive for, seek after." Just as it is necessary to diligently pursue a person in order to persecute him, so Paul urged Timothy to diligently pursue righteousness, faith, love, and peace. Paul was not referring to anything less than an intense pursuit — there is no lackadaisical following here.

Some Christians are frustrated because they do not experience all they think they should in the Christian life. Often this is because they settle down in the Christian life as if they were only going along for the ride rather than getting down to the business of pursuing that which is good.

We should make no mistake about the fact that Christ has fully paid sin's penalty and that we are completely delivered from condemnation by receiving Him as Savior (John 5:24). Also, we need to realize that we are complete in Christ and that we are to appropriate what He has made available to us. However, let us not overlook the personal discipline that Paul exercised in following that which was good. He emphasized in his letter to the Christians at Philippi, "Not that I have already obtained it, or have already become perfect, but I press on *[diōkō]* in order that I may lay hold of that for which also I was laid hold of by Christ Jesus. Brethren, I do not regard myself as having laid hold of it yet; but one thing I do: forgetting what lies behind and reaching forward to what lies ahead, I press on *[diōkō]* toward the goal for the prize of the upward call of God in Christ Jesus" (Philippians 3:12-14).

Although Paul realized his need was to appropriate what Christ had done for him, this never became a passive thing as far as his zeal in serving the Lord was concerned. Knowing that he was complete in Christ gave him a greater determination to expend every effort to know Christ and to make Him known. Because the truth of the grace of God had so captivated his life, Paul could do nothing less than give an all-out effort to pursue that which was good for his own life and to do that which would make it possible for others to know Christ.

How diligent are we in our pursuit of the things of God? Are we content with a casual reading of the Scriptures, or is there a desire to dig deeper so we might know more about Jesus Christ, who has done so much for us? When we attend church, do we let our minds drift from what is being said, or do we make a definite effort to concentrate on the things of God during that time?

When we appropriate more of what Christ has done for us in breaking sin's power over us, it will not result in passive understanding but in aggressive action to glorify Him.

22

Is Lust Always Bad?

The word *lust* as it is commonly used today — though it has other meanings — usually refers to intense sexual desire. This word is found in various translations of the Bible. It is usually a translation of the noun *epithumia* and its verb *epithumeō*. It is true that these words were sometimes used in referring to intense sexual desire. Commenting on the commandment "You shall not commit adultery" (Exodus 20:14), the Lord Jesus Christ said, " 'But I say to you, that everyone who looks on a woman to lust for her has committed adultery with her already in his heart' " (Matthew 5:28).

However, the words *epithumia* and *epithumeō* by themselves refer only to desire, usually strong desire. The context must determine whether it is a desire for good or a desire for evil. The verb, referring to a desire for good, is found in Luke 22:15, where Christ says to the apostles, " 'I have earnestly desired *[epithumeō]* to eat this Passover with you before I suffer.' " Thus, it is evident that these words can refer to a strong desire for that which is good. Of course, here it is translated "desire" rather than "lust." But this fact in itself helps us see the true meaning of the Greek words.

The apostle Paul used these words in their good sense: "But I am hard-pressed from both directions, having the desire *[epithu-*

mia] to depart and be with Christ, for that is very much better"
(Philippians 1:23). He also wrote: "But we, brethren, having been
bereft of you for a short while — in person, not in spirit — were
all the more eager with great desire *[epithumia]* to see your face" (1
Thessalonians 2:17). The good sense of *epithumeō* was used by
Paul in referring to a church office: "It is a trustworthy statement:
if any man aspires to the office of overseer, it is a fine work he desires *[epithumeō]* to do" (1 Timothy 3:1).

Even when *epithumia* and *epithumeō* are used in the bad sense,
they can have a far wider meaning than just intense sexual desire.
In His parable of the sower, Christ said, "And others are the ones
on whom seed was sown among the thorns; these are the ones
who have heard the word, and the worries of the world, and the
deceitfulness of riches, and the desires *[epithumia]* for other things
enter in and choke the word, and it becomes unfruitful" (Mark
4:18-19). These had a stronger desire for the things of the world
than for the things of God.

In talking to the unbelievers in His day, the Lord Jesus Christ
said, " 'You are of your father the devil, and you want to do the
desires *[epithumia]* of your father. He was a murderer from the beginning, and does not stand in the truth, because there is no truth
in him. Whenever he speaks a lie, he speaks from his own nature;
for he is a liar' " (John 8:44). Unbelievers are in Satan's control,
and they serve his desires.

The desires of the old nature are referred to as the "lust of the
flesh" (1 John 2:16). The desires of the old nature are in direct
conflict to the desires of the new nature in the believer. Paul
writes: "For the flesh sets its desire *[epithumeō]* against the Spirit,
and the Spirit against the flesh; for these are in opposition to one
another, so that you may not do the things that you please" (Galatians 5:17). The strong desires of the flesh are against the Spirit,
and the strong desires of the Spirit are against the flesh. The believer's formula for a victorious Christian life is given in the preceding verse: "Walk by the Spirit, and you will not carry out the
desire *[epithumia]* of the flesh."

23
Paid in Full

In His Sermon on the Mount, the Lord Jesus Christ said, " 'When therefore you give alms, do not sound a trumpet before you, as the hypocrites do in the synagogues and in the streets, that they may be honored by men. Truly I say to you, they have their reward in full' " (Matthew 6:2). In the last phrase, the word translated "have" is *apechō*. Although the meaning is clear from the English translation, Christ's statement has even greater force when viewed in its original setting. The word *apechō* was used in secular Greek as a technical expression in drawing up a receipt. In this sense it meant "paid in full."

When used in the New Testament, *apechō* does not always have this technical meaning, but in several passages it is apparent that the technical meaning is intended. Such is the case in Matthew 6:2. Those who do their alms to be seen of men are paid in full by the praise they receive from men. When they are seen of men, it is as if they were handed a receipt marked "Paid in Full." They should never expect to receive further reward for what they have done.

The subject of verse 2 is the giving of alms. The word translated "alms" is *eleēmosunē*. It is from this Greek word we get our term "eleemosynary," which refers to that which is related to, or supported by, charity.

Whether we are giving to the Lord's work or to a humanitarian organization supported by charity, if we give in order to be seen of men, we should consider that we have been paid in full for what we have done. We should not expect further reward from the Lord if our chief concern in giving was to be seen of men.

In verse 5 of this same chapter, the Lord speaks concerning prayer: " 'And when you pray, you are not to be as the hypocrites; for they love to stand and pray in the synagogues and on the street corners, in order to be seen by men. Truly I say to you, they have their reward in full.' " The last sentence of this verse is exactly the same as the last phrase of verse 2 and has the same technical meaning of being "paid in full."

Public prayer usually presents a difficulty to every Christian. The believer realizes he is actually talking to God, and yet he feels he must be so conscious of his choice of words because others are listening. However, the New Testament encourages public prayer, and we should not avoid it because of our concern for what others may think. On the other hand, if we pray only because we are in public and want to be heard of men, then we have been "paid in full" and should expect no futher reward.

Verse 16 of the same chapter comments on fasting: " 'And whenever you fast, do not put on a gloomy face as the hypocrites do, for they neglect their appearance in order to be seen fasting by men. Truly I say to you, they have their reward in full.' " Again the same phrase is used with the same meaning, but it is applied to a different subject.

Whether or not we should fast today is debatable. Men of God take various positions on the question. But at least in a general sense this verse can be applied to those of us who are living for the Lord today. Just as the hypocrites who fasted were concerned that they might be seen of men and have sympathy for their sacrifice, so present-day believers are sometimes guilty of wanting others to sympathize with them in what they have sacrificed. Some believers emphasize what important positions they could have had in the world as unbelievers. Others tell of the pleasures of the world they have given up in order to live for Christ. Still others want people to know what a sacrifice it is to be a missionary or to be involved in full-time Christian work. Whenever we are guilty of playing on the sympathies of others, we need to realize that we have been "paid in full" by the sympathies and praises received from men.

No Christian who knows the corruptness of the human heart would ever have fantasies about what he might have been apart from Jesus Christ. No Christian who has experienced the peace of God would ever be jealous of those who are "enjoying" the temporary pleasures of sin. No one who has grasped the meaning of the grace of God in his own life would ever call it "sacrifice" to spend his life telling others that Jesus Christ died for them also.

Because of what Jesus Christ has done for us, it should be our desire to please Him in everything we do. When this is the case, our reward will not all be received here on earth. When we see Jesus Christ face to face we shall be "paid in full."

24
Appearance of Evil

Have you known of some people who would not drink a soft drink from a bottle because alcoholic beverages also come in bottles and drinking the soft drink would have an "appearance of evil"? Or have you known of some who would not watch a Christian film, shown in a church, because non-Christians have used movies to show all kinds of perversion; thus, watching the Christian film would have "an appearance of evil"?

Those who have such views usually base them on 1 Thessalonians 5:22: "Abstain from every appearance of evil" (KJV). This verse is commonly interpreted as reading: "Abstain from everything that might appear to be evil." The question that must be answered in properly interpreting the verse is whether the verse refers to doing things that are good but might appear to be evil or whether it refers to evil, which appears in different forms.

The word translated "appearance" in the KJV is *eidos*. This Greek word occurs five times in the New Testament: Luke 3:22; 9:29; John 5:37; 2 Corinthians 5:7; and 1 Thessalonians 5:22. It is closely associated with the word that means "to see," and thus *eidos* has to do with that which strikes the eye or is seen. In secular Greek during New Testament times it commonly had to do with "form," because a form is something that can be seen. The word was found in the heading of a list of personal property and meant "list of effects." It was a listing or itemizing of that which was seen.

It is also interesting to note that the word *idol* was a compound Greek word, one part meaning "that which is seen" and the other part meaning "whole, entire." A person bowing down to an idol is giving himself to that which is wholly seen. But in a broader sense, whenever those living in the twentieth century give themselves to that which is seen (materialism) instead of to that which is not seen (God and spiritual verities), they are idol worshipers just as much as those who bow down to idols of wood and stone.

Because the word *eidos* has to do with "form," a more accurate translation of 1 Thessalonians 5:22 is rendered in the NASB: "Abstain from every form of evil." Romans 14 and 1 Corinthians 8 deal specifically with stronger Christians who do things which cause weaker Christians to stumble. It is true that the Christian needs to guard against doing anything that may not be evil in itself but which may appear to be evil and become a stumbling block to others. However, in 1 Thessalonians 5:21-22 the emphasis is on holding to that which is good and keeping away from that which is evil. Paul wrote that the Christians in Thessalonica should "examine everything carefully."

The word translated "examine" is *dokimazō*, which means "put to the test" or "prove by testing." This word is used in 1 Peter 1:7, where it refers to gold that has been "tested by fire." Just as in the testing of gold the impurities were removed and the gold kept, Paul was telling the Thessalonians to test everything and to hold to that which was good while abstaining from that which was evil — "every form of evil." Regardless of how spiritual a church or a ministry may be, evil can appear in many forms. The Christian's need is to be discerning so that he might abstain (keep away) from evil regardless of the form in which it appears.

25
Kinds of Love

We commonly use the word *love* in many ways. We have one kind of love for our marriage partner, another kind of love for our children, another kind for our friends, and still another kind for various things in our lives.

In Greek, different words were used for *love* which showed the particular meaning intended. During New Testament times there were actually four words in use that emphasized different aspects of love. However, only two of these appear in the New Testament.

The word *eros,* which does not appear in the Greek New Testament, was predominantly used in referring to physical love. Eventually this word became associated with the lower side of love, especially in regard to passion. It is from this word that we get the word *erotic,* which means "of, devoted to, or tending to arouse, sexual love or desire."

Another word in common use at that time was *storgē,* which had mostly to do with affection within the family relationship. Although it was used for the love a ruler might have for his people, it was mainly used in referring to the love of parents for their children and children for their parents.

This word is not used in the New Testament either, but words derived from it are. For instance, Romans 12:10 says, "Be devoted to one another in brotherly love; give preference to one another in honor." The words "be devoted to" are translated from a word related to *storgē.*

One of the ways of forming a negative in Greek is by prefixing a word with the letter *a.* We have this in English in such words as "asocial." The negative of *storgē* is *astorgē,* and this word appears in 2 Timothy 3:3. In this verse Paul is describing some of the characteristics of the last days. He says it will be a time when people will be "unloving." Family affection will be at a low ebb. Even today, with the increase in divorce, spouse and child abuse, and perverse sexuality, one can see this prophecy being fulfilled. The negative, *astorgē,* is also translated "unloving" in Romans 1:31.

Another word commonly used in Bible times — and is frequently found in the Greek New Testament — is *philos.* This word especially emphasizes affection that grows out of mutual response. It is primarily an emotional and reciprocal love. This was the word that Mary and Martha used when they sent a message to the Lord telling Him about Lazarus. They said, " 'Lord, behold, he whom You love is sick' " (John 11:3). The word "love" in this verse is the verb form of *philos.*

The word that especially expresses God's love and the kind of love Christians should have is *agapē.* This word has to do not only with the emotions but also with the will. It is the kind of love that loves even when there is no response. This is the word used for love in Romans 5:5-6: "And hope does not disappoint, because the love *[agapē]* of God has been poured out within our hearts through the Holy Spirit who was given to us. For while we were still helpless, at the right time Christ died for the ungodly." Although mankind was the enemy of Christ, He loved us even when there was no response, and He died on the cross for us.

It is this kind of love the apostle John referred to when he said, "Beloved, let us love one another, for love is from God; and every one who loves is born of God and knows God. The one who does not love does not know God, for God is love" (1 John 4:7-8).

The only way a person can have the kind of love that loves even when there is no response is to know Jesus Christ as Savior. This is the kind of love He has, and when we receive Him as Savior, He comes to live in us and works out this love through us. This kind of love is more than an emotion — it is a deliberate conviction of mind that determines a way of life. It involves an act of the will.

The Christian is not only to love those in his family, other Christians, and neighbors, but he is also to love his enemies. The Lord Jesus Christ Himself said, "But I say to you who hear, love *[agapē]* your enemies, do good to those who hate you" (Luke 6:27). This kind of love results only from an act of the will, because certainly it is not an emotion or reciprocal affection where an enemy is concerned. It means that regardless of what the enemy does to us, we will seek only to bring about the highest good for him. We will be kind and will seek to win him to Christ, because we know this is his greatest need, even if he does not realize it.

26
The Believer's Title Deed

Hebrews 11:1 says, "Now faith is the assurance of things hoped for, the conviction of things not seen." The Greek word that forms the basis for the word "assurance" in this translation is *hupostasis*. This is actually a compound word made up of the preposition *hupo*, meaning "under," and a word derived from *histēmi*, which means "to stand." Hence, *hupostasis* refers to that which stands under anything.

This Greek word appears in only two books of the New Testament: 2 Corinthians (9:4; 11:17) and Hebrews (1:3; 3:14; 11:1). In 2 Corinthians 9:4 it is translated "confidence" (associated with boasting) and in 2 Corinthians 11:17 it is translated "confidence of boasting." The element of confidence is derived from this word inasmuch as it emphasizes a foundation, or that which stands under. Because facts supported his boasts, what Paul said could be spoken of as "confidence of boasting."

Hebrews 1:3 refers to the Lord Jesus Christ of whom it states: "He is the the radiance of His glory and the exact representation of His nature *[hupostasis]*, and upholds all things by the word of His power. When He had made purification of sins, He sat down at the right hand of the Majesty on high." *Hupostasis* emphasizes that which stands underneath, or substance. In Hebrews 3:14 the word is used to emphasize that which underlies one's confidence or assurance: "For we have become partakers of Christ, if we hold fast to the beginning of our assurance *[hupostasis]* firm until the end."

With these other uses as background, and with the knowledge that the word emphasizes that which stands under or supports something, a new dimension is added to our understanding of Hebrews 11:1: "Now faith is the assurance of things hoped for." In secular Greek of New Testament times, *hupostasis* was used in the sense of "agreement of sale." Thus it conveyed the idea of evidence of ownership. It would be valid, therefore, to translate Hebrews 11:1: "Now faith is the title deed of things hoped for." Faith is simply taking God at His word and acting accordingly. This kind of faith is the present title deed to what we will receive from God in the future.

The last phrase of Hebrews 11:1, "the conviction of things not seen," further expresses the thought of the first part of the verse. Whereas the phrase "things hoped for" refers to the future, the phrase "things not seen" can refer to past, present, and future. The person who has taken God at His word concerning sin and the need to receive Christ as Savior should have no difficulty in taking God at His word when He describes things that are not seen. The object of the believer's faith is God, as described in the Bible. Because this is so, there need be no lack of assurance concerning the things hoped for. We already have the title deed!

27
The Believer's Help

The apostle John used a Greek word in his writings that no other inspired writer of the Scriptures used. This word is *paraklētos*. It is from this word that we get our term *paraclete*. In all, John used the word five times: four in his gospel and once in his first epistle.

The word *paraklētos* is actually a combination of two Greek words. The first half of the word is the preposition *para*, which had the common meaning "alongside of." This Greek preposition is commonly found in the English language in such words as "paragraph" (to write alongside) and "parallel" (alongside one another). The other Greek word from which *parakletos* was formed was *kaleō*, which commonly meant "to call." From these separate words it is apparent that the compound Greek word *paraklētos* referred to one called alongside.

In his gospel, the apostle John used the word four times (14:16, 26; 15:26; 16:7). In each case the word refers to the Holy Spirit. In chapter 14, John is recording the words of Christ, who said, " 'And I will ask the Father, and He will give you another Helper *[paraklētos]*, that He may be with you forever' " (v. 16). The disciples were concerned about Christ's statements that He was going to the Father, but Christ assured them that when He went to the Father, He would send them "another Helper." The word "another" is *allos,* which means "another of the same kind" — the same kind as Christ had been to them. Thus the ministry of the Holy Spirit would aid the disciples in the same way Jesus had aided them while He was in their midst physically.

The Holy Spirit is One called alongside to help, and although this help includes consoling, it also includes many other things. This is evident from the other references in John's gospel that refer to the Holy Spirit as the *paraklētos.* Christ said, " 'But the Helper *[paraklētos],* the Holy Spirit, whom the Father will send in My name, He will teach you all things, and bring to your remembrance all that I said to you' " (14:26).

The Holy Spirit was to help the disciples by reminding them of the things Christ had spoken to them. This is also emphasized in 15:26:" 'When the Helper *[paraklētos]* comes, whom I will send to you from the Father, that is the Spirit of truth, who proceeds from the Father, He will bear witness of Me.' "

John 16 further delineates the ministry of the Holy Spirit. Christ said, " 'But I tell you the truth, it is to your advantage that I go away; for if I do not go away, the Helper *[paraklētos]* shall not come to you; but if I go, I will send Him to you' " (v. 7).

Christ then went on to say what the ministry of the Holy Spirit would be when He came: " 'And He, when He comes, will convict the world concerning sin, and righteousness, and judgment; concerning sin, because they do not believe in Me; and concerning righteousness, because I go to the Father, and you no longer behold Me; and concerning judgment, because the ruler of this world has been judged' " (vv. 8-11.).

It should be remembered that the Holy Spirit is not seeking to draw attention to Himself but is seeking to direct attention to the Lord Jesus Christ. This is evident from what Christ said: " 'I have many more things to say to you, but you cannot bear them now. But when He, the Spirit of truth, comes, He will guide you into all the truth; for He will not speak on His own initiative, but whatever He hears, He will speak; and He will disclose to you what is to come. He shall glorify Me; for He shall take of Mine, and shall disclose it to you. All things that the Father has are Mine; therefore I said, that He takes of Mine, and will disclose it to you' " (vv. 12-15). Therefore, the greatest evidence that the Holy Spirit has been able to accomplish His purpose in a person's life is that the person is completely taken up with the Lord Jesus Christ. It is important that we know how the Holy Spirit works so we may be controlled by Him, but the Holy Spirit does not desire our attention to be upon Him but rather upon Jesus Christ.

The apostle John used the word *paraklētos* once in his first epistle, and there it clearly refers to the Lord Jesus Christ. John wrote to believers: "My little children, I am writing these things to you that you may not sin. And if anyone sins, we have an Advocate *[paraklētos]* with the Father, Jesus Christ the righteous" (2:1). John went on to describe the Lord Jesus Christ by saying, "And He Himself is the propitiation [satisfaction] for our sins; and not for ours only, but also for those of the whole world" (v. 2).

When Jesus Christ died on the cross for the sins of the world, He completely satisfied the righteous demands of God the Father. Therefore, having received Jesus Christ as Savior, we have an advocate, or helper, who represents us before the heavenly Father. How wonderful it is to realize that the grace of God is so marvelous that He has provided Jesus Christ as our advocate and intercessor in heaven and has given us the Holy Spirit to be our helper here on earth!

28

Ransomed Forever

As the believer grows in his knowledge of the Scriptures and of Christ, he realizes he will never be able to fully understand redemption. But as he sees what his redemption cost God and what the results have been in his own life, his heart responds in worship to God.

There are three words in the Greek New Testament that especially relate to the subject of redemption. They are *agorazō, exagorazō,* and *lutroō.*

The word *agorazō* appears thirty-one times in the Greek New Testament. It was used in the secular Greek of New Testament times to mean "to buy in the marketplace, to purchase." It comes from the word *agora,* which means "marketplace." Hence, *agorazō* had to do with buying or purchasing in the marketplace.

In New Testament times, *agorazō* was also used in reference to the buying of slaves. The New Testament writers saw mankind as slaves to sin and used this word to show that Christ has bought us. The word is used in 1 Corinthians 6:20, where the apostle Paul writes: "For you have been bought *[agorazō]* with a price: therefore glorify God in your body." Paul also wrote: "You were bought *[agorazō]* with a price; do not become slaves of men" (7:23).

In order for anything to be bought, a price must be paid. Refer-

ring to the Tribulation saints, Revelation 5:9 tells of the price that
had to be paid for them as well as for all believers: "And they sang
a new song, saying, 'Worthy art Thou to take the book, and to
break its seals; for Thou wast slain, and didst purchase *[agorazō]*
for God with Thy blood men from every tribe and tongue and
people and nation.' " The redemption of man cost Jesus His life,
for it was necessary for Him to shed His blood in order for mankind to be purchased from the slavery of sin.

Another word that relates the subject of redemption is *exagorazō*. The "ex" prefix on *agorazō* is a preposition that emphasizes
separation. Thus, this word emphasizes that which is bought *out of*
the marketplace, whereas *agorazō* emphasizes the buying *in* the
marketplace. In *agorazō* we see that Christ paid the price for our
sin, and in *exagorazō* we see that He has taken us out of the marketplace of sin. He did not buy us to leave us under the domina-
tion of sin. *Exagorazō* appears four times in the New Testament.
Galatians 3:13 says, "Christ redeemed *[exagorazō]* us from the
curse of the Law, having become a curse for us — for it is written,
'Cursed is everyone who hangs on a tree.' " The word is also related to the law in Galatians 4:5, which tells us that Christ came "in
order that He might redeem *[exagorazō]* those who were under the
Law, that we might receive the adoption as sons." Christ has taken
us out of the marketplace of sin and out from under the dominion
of the law.

Exagorazō is used concerning time and opportunities. Ephesians
5:16 says, "Making the most *[exagorazō]* of your time, because the
days are evil." Colossians 4:5 states a similar truth: "Conduct yourselves with wisdom toward outsiders, making the most *[exagorazō]*
of the opportunity."

The word *lutroō* is another word of significance in the study of
redemption. It appears three times in the Greek New Testament.
Also the noun form of *lutroō* means "ransom," and *lutroō* means
"to release on receipt of ransom" or "to deliver." In this word we
see the emphasis on our release from slavery to sin because of the
price Christ paid.

Lutroō occurs in Luke 24:21: "But we were hoping that it was
He who was going to redeem *[lutroō]* Israel. Indeed, besides all
this, it is the third day since these things happened." In this verse

the emphasis is clearly on deliverance because of a price that was paid.

Deliverance is also seen in Titus 2:14, which says of Christ, "Who gave Himself for us, that He might redeem *[lutroō]* us from every lawless deed and purify for Himself a people for His own possession, zealous for good deeds." The third appearance of *lut-roō* is in 1 Peter 1:18: "Knowing that you were not redeemed *[lut-roō]* with perishable things like silver or gold from your futile way of life inherited from your forefathers."

How wonderful it is to realize that Christ not only paid the full price for our sin but that He also took us out from under the do-minion of sin and set us free. Having received Him as Savior, we are now free to please Him in all that we do.

29
Yield!

A key chapter on the victorious Christian life is Romans 6. From this chapter it is evident that the believer is to know certain things (vv. 6-10), is to reckon them to be so (vv. 11-12), and is to yield himself to God (v. 13). Verse 13 says, "Neither yield ye your members as instruments of unrighteousness unto sin: but yield yourselves unto God, as those that are alive from the dead, and your members as instruments of righteousness unto God" (KJV). Verse 16 further emphasizes the matter of yielding: "Know ye not, that to whom ye yield yourselves servants to obey, his servants ye are to whom ye obey; whether of sin unto death, or of obedience unto righteousness?" (KJV). And verse 19 adds, "I speak after the manner of men because of the infirmity of your flesh: for as ye have yielded your members servants to uncleanness and to iniquity unto iniquity; even so now yield your members servants to righteousness unto holiness" (KJV).

What is involved in yielding to the Lord? Because the word *yield* in our common usage has a meaning of "surrender," it is often interpreted in only this passive sense when used in the Scriptures. But there is much more involved in the word.

Although technically there are two different Greek words used in Romans 6 that are translated by a form of the word *yield* in the

KJV, both Greek words have the same basic idea, as one seems to be only a later development of the other. The older word, *paristēmi*, literally means "to stand beside." Other related meanings would be "to place beside" and "to put at the disposal of." We are helped in our understanding of the word "yield" in Romans 6:13 when we realize it is the same word that is translated "present" in Romans 12:1: "I urge you therefore, brethren, by the mercies of God, to present *[paristēmi]* your bodies a living and holy sacrifice, acceptable to God, which is your spiritual service of worship." Thus, Romans 6:13 and 12:1 are emphasizing the same truth. The NASB uses "present" in Romans 6:13 as well as Romans 12:1 to convey the meaning of the Greek words involved.

Paristēmi was also used of servants, who "stood by" to do their masters' bidding. When Jesus was taken before the high priest after being betrayed by Judas, He answered the high priest in a way that displeased one of the officers who was listening. "And when He [Jesus] had said this, one of the officers standing by *[paristēmi]* gave Jesus a blow, saying, 'Is that the way You answer the high priest?' " (John 18:22). The officer who was "standing by" was committed to carrying out the will of those who had authority over him. Such a person had not only yielded his will to serve the desires of others, but he was ready to aggressively carry out the will of his superiors.

The word *paristēmi* is also used concerning the angel Gabriel. When he appeared to Zacharias, he said, " 'I am Gabriel, who stands *[paristēmi]* in the presence of God; and I have been sent to speak to you, and to bring you this good news' " (Luke 1:19). Gabriel was at God's disposal and had been sent to Zacharias to announce that Zacharias and Elizabeth were to have a son.

Thus, when a believer yields to the Lord, it is more than just a "giving up" of his own plans and desires — it is placing himself at God's disposal to carry out God's will. It is true that only God can effectively accomplish a spiritual work, but He does it through believers.

When we make such statements as "I didn't do anything; I just let Christ do it all," we must be sure that our listeners know what we mean. Christ lives within every believer, as the apostle Paul frequently emphasized, and Christ's desire is to live His life through the believer. We are to be yielded to Him in the sense that we present ourselves to God. We do not give up our wills, but we are to use our wills to carry out His will. We are to put ourselves at His disposal so He can manifest His life through us and reach the world through us.

We have all that we need in Jesus Christ. Our responsibility now is to claim it and to go forward in aggressively carrying out His will.

30
Hospitality

In the mad rush of our age it is difficult to find time to entertain friends. Evenings are often scheduled with meetings or work that needs to be done. When there finally is a free evening, it is nice to spend it doing something with the family or just relaxing on one's own. So it is obviously difficult to work in time to have friends over occasionally for a few hours of fellowship.

When we think of showing hospitality or of being hospitable, we usually have in mind the entertaining of our friends. Certainly this is included, but when the Bible talks about hospitality, it includes more than entertaining friends.

The apostle Paul reminded the Christians at Rome that they should be "practicing hospitality" (Romans 12:13). The Greek word translated "hospitality" is *philoxenia*. This word is composed from two Greek words. One of the words is *philos*, which means "friend" and is related to one of the Greek words for "love" (see chapter 25). The other word is *xenos*, which means "stranger." Thus the word *philoxenia* refers to one who is a "stranger lover."

The hospitality to which the apostle Paul referred included far more than having friends over for the evening — it meant entertaining strangers as guests. Nor did Paul see this as an easy thing to do, for the word translated "practicing" is *diōkō*, which means "to pursue" (see chapter 21). It takes planning and intense pursuit if we are to entertain strangers as we should.

Hebrews 13:2 shows the rewards of entertaining strangers: "Do not neglect to show hospitality to strangers, for by this some have entertained angels without knowing it." A person who may be a stranger to us can be a messenger of God in that he brings something to our attention that we have not previously considered. Comments made by a stranger might well affect our entire lives as God uses those comments to give us a greater vision for His work and the world.

So important is the entertaining of strangers that the apostle Paul gave it as one of the requirements for a church officer: "An overseer, then, must be above reproach, the husband of one wife, temperate, prudent, respectable, hospitable *[philoxenos]*, able to teach" (1 Timothy 3:2). One who is to be an overseer in the church must, among other things, be a "stranger lover." Christians will not have the impact we should have on society unless we are really concerned about strangers; we must have a genuine love for people.

Paul emphasized this same requirement to Titus when he wrote: "For the overseer must be above reproach as God's steward, not self-willed, not quick-tempered, not addicted to wine, not pugnacious, not fond of sordid gain, but hospitable *[philoxenos]*, loving what is good, sensible, just, devout, self-controlled" (Titus 1:7-8).

The apostle Peter wrote: "Be hospitable *[philoxenos]* to one another without complaint" (1 Peter 4:9). That friends as well as strangers are included in hospitality is evident from the previous verse: "Above all, keep fervent in your love for one another, because love covers a multitude of sins."

Christ said, "By this all men will know that you are My disciples, if you have love for one another" (John 13:35). This includes showing our love not only to our friends but also to strangers. Are we "stranger lovers," or do we love only those in our close circle of friends?

31

Does God Punish Believers?

When referring to the fact of God's bringing adversity into a believer's life, various translations use the words "chasten" or "chastisement," and "punish" or "punishment" in rendering the same verses. Three different but related Greek words are involved. The noun *paideia* occurs six times in the New Testament. The NASB translates it "discipline" in Ephesians 6:4 and Hebrews 12:5, 7, 8, 11; "training" in 2 Timothy 3:16. Basically, *paideia* refers to "upbringing, training, instruction." The chief idea of this word seems to be that of discipline, and it is closely associated with training and education.

The verb *paideuō* occurs thirteen times in the New Testament. The NASB translates it "discipline" in 1 Corinthians 11:32, Hebrews 12:6, 7, 10, Revelation 3:19; "punish" in 2 Corinthians 6:9, Luke 23:16, 22; "correct" in 2 Timothy 2:25; "instruct" in Titus 2:12; "taught" in 1 Timothy 1:20; "educated" in Acts 22:3; and "was educated" in Acts 7:22. As a verb, it has to do with the act of bringing up, instructing, training, and educating. Like the noun *paideia*, the verb *paideuō* involves correction, because that is part of the process of training or educating.

The person who did the upbringing or training was referred to as a *paideutēs*. This word occurs twice in the New Testament and is translated in the NASB as "corrector" in Romans 2:20 and "to discipline" in Hebrews 12:9.

Altogether, these three Greek words — *paideia, paideuō,* and *paideutēs* — appear twenty-one times in the New Testament. Eight of those occurrences are in Hebrews 12:5-11. This passage states:

"And you have forgotten the exhortation which is addressed to you as sons, 'My son, do not regard lightly the discipline *[paideia]* of the Lord, nor faint when you are reproved by Him; for those whom the Lord loves He disciplines *[paideuō]*, and He scourges every son whom He receives.' It is for discipline that you endure; God deals with you as with sons; for what son is there whom his father does not discipline *[paideuō]*? But if you are without discipline *[paideia]*, of which all have become partakers, then you are illegitimate children and not sons. Furthermore, we had earthly fathers to discipline *[paideutēs]* us, and we respected them; shall we not much rather be subject to the Father of spirits, and live? For they disciplined *[paideuō]* us for a short time as seemed best to them, but He disciplines *[paideuō]* us for our good, that we may share His holiness. All discipline *[paideia]* for the moment seems not to be joyful, but sorrowful; yet to those who have been trained by it, afterwards it yields the peaceful fruit of righteousness."

To some extent "chastise" and "punish" are interchangeable, yet each seems to have its own emphasis. "Punish" is more negative in that it involves correction for wrongdoing. "Chastise," or "discipline," is more positive in that its purpose is to motivate to better behavior. Certainly "discipline" would include a penalty for wrongdoing, but it has a teaching purpose — it is not an end in itself.

In his book *Reality Therapy*, psychiatrist William Glasser distinguishes between discipline and punishment. In the chapter entitled "The Treatment of Seriously Delinquent Adolescent Girls" Dr. Glasser writes: "Girls are willing to accept discipline but not punishment; they differentiate between the two by seeing whether the disciplining person shows anger and gets satisfaction by exercising power" (p. 78).

God does not chastise believers because He receives satisfaction from it or wants to display His power; He chastises us because He wants to accomplish something in our lives that will be for our good and His glory. God disciplines and allows adversity into our lives because He knows "that the proof of your faith, being more precious than gold which is perishable" and that it is through the trial of our faith that we will be "found to result in praise and glory and honor at the revelation of Jesus Christ" (1 Peter 1:7).

Closely associated with the fact that "God causes all things to work together for good" to believers is the fact that He has predestinated believers to "become conformed to the image of His Son" (Romans 8:28-29). The purpose of God's discipline is to conform us to the image of Jesus Christ.

Above all, we should realize that God does not punish believers in the sense of condemning. Jesus Christ has taken all our condemnation upon Himself. The Lord Jesus assured believers, " 'He who hears My word, and believes Him who sent Me, has eternal life, and does not come into judgment, but has passed out of death into life' " (John 5:24).

We are not serving an angry God who loves to punish us every time we fail; rather, we are serving a God of grace who has borne all our condemnation and who now wants to live His life through us. True, He corrects us for wrongdoing, but His purpose is to bring about more responsible behavior from us, which will be glorifying to Him.

32
Needed: More Mimics

We get our word *type* from the word *tupos,* which occurs sixteen times in the Greek New Testament. At first, the word was used to refer to a strike, or blow, and later came to emphasize the mark or impression left by a blow. The word also had the idea of "pattern," for the mark left was a pattern of that which delivered the blow. Just as an official seal, such as that used by a corporation or an educational institution, leaves its pattern or impression, the person who is a *tupos* leaves his impression on others, so they reflect him.

It is in this sense that a believer is to be a model, or pattern, for other believers. Paul told the Philippian believers, "Brethren, join in following my example *[tupos]*" (Philippians 3:17). The Philippian believers were to pattern their lives after Paul and other mature believers. In fact, Paul sometimes did things specifically for the purpose of being an example. When he was in Thessalonica, he purposely earned his own living in order to set an example for believers. Reminding them later of this fact, Paul said, "Nor did we eat anyone's bread without paying for it, but with labor and hardship we kept working night and day so that we might not be a burden to any of you; not because we do not have the right [authority] to this, but in order to offer ourselves as a model for you, that you might follow our example *[tupos]*" (2 Thessalonians 3:8-9). The apostle Peter exhorted those in positions of spiritual leadership, "Shepherd the flock of God among you, exercising oversight not under compulsion, but voluntarily, according to the will of God; and not for sordid gain, but with eagerness; nor yet as lording it over those allotted to your charge, but proving to be examples *[tupos]* to the flock" (1 Peter 5:2-3). Just as we reap what we sow, those to whom we minister will reflect us. It is important, therefore, that we be good examples for them to follow.

The Scriptures also emphasize the importance of *following* good examples. The apostle Paul wrote to the Corinthian believers: "I exhort you therefore, be imitators of me" (1 Corinthians 4:16). The word translated "imitators" is *mimētēs,* from which we get our word *mimic.*

Although the word *mimic* is often thought of in a bad sense, in the New Testament this Greek word was always used in a good sense. Thus, Paul was exhorting the Corinthians to mimic his way of life. Paul made clear, however, why it was safe to make such an exhortation — he was mimicking Jesus Christ. Paul said, "Be imitators *[mimētēs]* of me, just as I also am of Christ" (1 Corinthians 11:1). When we make it our chief goal to imitate Jesus Christ in our daily living, it will be safe for us to urge others to imitate us. Paul was not saying that he never made mistakes, but he was encouraging others to make Christ central in their thinking, even as he had in his.

Paul reminded the believers in Thessalonica, "You also became imitators *[mimētēs]* of us and of the Lord, having received the word in much tribulation with the joy of the Holy Spirit, so that you became an example *[tupos]* to all the believers in Macedonia and in Achaia" (1 Thessalonians 1:6-7). Because the believers in Thessalonica had imitated, or mimicked, the Lord and also mature believers, they became models for others. Thus, we see that one must pattern his life after the Lord before he can become a good pattern for others to follow.

Our need, then, is to saturate our lives with the Word of God so that we might know how to properly imitate the Lord in any situation. At the same time, we will become good examples for others to follow.

33
Building Spiritual Houses

One frequently hears the expression "building up Christians in the faith." This is a scriptural expression, because it is based on many New Testament verses, especially those written by the apostle Paul.

In New Testament times, the common word for "building," or "building up," was *oikodomeō*. This verb was formed by joining *oikos*, meaning "house," and *demo*, meaning "to build." Thus, the word *oikodomeō* literally meant "to build a house," but it was applied to building in general.

The apostle Paul chose this common word for "building" and applied it to Christians. In 1 Corinthians he used both the noun *oikodomē*, meaning "building," and the verb *oikodomeō*, meaning "to build."

Paul told the Corinthian believers, "You are God's...building [*oikodomē*]" (3:9). Concerning what he had done for the Corinthians, Paul said, "As a wise master builder, I laid a foundation, and another is building [*oikodomeō*] upon it. For no man can lay a foundation other than the one which is laid, which is Jesus Christ" (vv. 10-11). Paul had told the Corinthians about Jesus Christ, and those who responded by receiving Him as Savior were said to have had the foundation laid in their lives. Everything else of spiritual value had to be laid on that foundation, Jesus Christ.

Paul then referred to those who would be building on the lives of the Corinthian believers when he said, "Now if any man builds [*oikodomeō*] upon the foundation with gold, silver, precious stones, wood, hay, straw, each man's work will become evident; for the day will show it, because it is to be revealed with fire; and the fire itself will test the quality of each man's work" (vv. 12-13).

This passage of Scripture is commonly explained as teaching that the person who stands before the Lord will be rewarded for the good in his life. Paul seems to be emphasizing, however, that when one believer stands before the Lord to have his life evaluated, others will be rewarded according to the way they built on that believer's life. Other passages of Scripture indicate that believers will stand before the Lord and be rewarded for what they have done for Him (2 Corinthians 5:10), but the emphasis in 1 Corinthians 3 is placed on what one person has done in another person's life. When the building is evaluated, the builder will be rewarded according to the quality of work he has built on the foundation, Jesus Christ.

One of Paul's major reasons for writing 1 Corinthians was to get the Corinthian believers to be more concerned about other believers. Therefore, he emphasized building on the foundation in others' lives.

The Corinthian believers were carnal; that is, they were more concerned about pleasing themselves than about pleasing Christ (3:1-4). They insisted on having their own rights rather than being concerned for others.

Selfishness was the main problem in the case Paul dealt with in chapter 8. Some believers insisted on doing what they knew was technically right, even though they were being stumbling blocks to weaker Christians. Paul reminded the Corinthian believers, "Knowledge makes arrogant, but love edifies [*oikodomeō*]" (v. 1).

Paul warned the Corinthian believers that by demanding their own rights, they were doing the wrong kind of building in the lives of weaker Christians. He told them, "For if someone sees you, who have knowledge, dining in an idol's temple, will not his conscience, if he is weak, be strengthened [*oikodomeō*] to eat things sacrificed to idols" (v. 10). Certainly, a believer who builds in the wrong way in another person's life will not receive a reward for what he has done. Unwise actions by believers can cause spiritual shipwreck to those who are weak in the faith. When we are motivated by love, we will not want to cause another person to stumble in his Christian walk. Paul emphasized the seriousness of causing others to stumble when he said, "And thus, by sinning against the brethren and wounding their conscience when it is weak, you sin against Christ" (v. 12).

Touching on the Christian's liberty in things not specifically prohibited by God's Word, Paul said, "All things are lawful, but not all things are profitable. All things are lawful, but not all things edify *[oikodomeō]*" (10:23). In the realm of Christian liberty, our concern should be to do that which encourages other Christians in the faith. When we insist on our own rights and flaunt our liberty, we are not manifesting the fruit of the indwelling Holy Spirit.

Other occurrences of *oikodomeō* and *oikodomē* are found in 1 Corinthians 14, where Paul deals with the specific problem of speaking in tongues. Here again, the Corinthian Christians were not considerate of the needs of other believers. They were far more concerned about exercising the gifts of the Spirit than they were about demonstrating the fruit of the Spirit. Paul told them, "But one who prophesies speaks to men for edification *[oikodomē]* and exhortation and consolation. One who speaks in a tongue edifies *[oikodomeō]* himself; but one who prophesies edifies *[oikodomeo]* the church" (vv. 3-4).

It does not seem that Paul was commending the believers for edifying themselves by speaking in tongues; rather, he was reprimanding them for not being concerned about edifying the church, or other believers. Paul went on to tell them, "Now I wish that you all spoke in tongues, but even more that you would prophesy; and greater is one who prophesies than one who speaks in tongues, unless he interprets, so that the church may receive edifying *[oikodomē]*" (v. 5).

Paul emphasized a concern for others when he wrote: "So also you, since you are zealous of spiritual gifts, seek to abound for the edification *[oikodomē]* of the church" (v. 12). The major concern when believers assemble is that everything that is done should result in encouraging and building up one another in the faith. For believers to be edified, they must understand what is being said. To those who were so concerned about speaking in tongues even when others could not understand, Paul said, "For you are giving thanks well enough, but the other man is not edified *[oikodomeō]*" (v. 17).

The key phrase of 1 Corinthians 14 may well be Paul's statement in verse 26: "Let all things be done for edification *[oikodomē]*."

34

Is Fear from God?

The seasoned apostle Paul told young Timothy, "For God has not given us a spirit of timidity, but of power and love and discipline" (2 Timothy 1:7).

This verse is difficult to understand when one remembers what the Scriptures say about fear. Proverbs 9:10 states, "The fear of the Lord is the beginning of wisdom, and the knowledge of the Holy One is understanding." Exodus 23:27 says, "I will send My terror ahead of you, and throw into confusion all the people among whom you come, and I will make all your enemies turn their backs to you."

With verses such as these, which clearly indicate that fear can have its origin in God, how does one explain 2 Timothy 1:7: "For God has not given us a spirit of timidity"? The answer is found in an understanding of the Greek word that is translated "timidity."

When Paul assured Timothy that the attitude of timidity did not originate with God, he used the word *deilia*. In this exact form, this is the only time *deilia* occurs in the New Testament. However, other closely related words are used. They are *deiliaō* (John 14:27) and *deilos* (Matthew 8:26; Mark 4:40; Revelation 21:8).

Deiliaō is translated "nor let it be fearful" in John 14:27, which records the words of Jesus: " 'Peace I leave with you, My peace I give to you; not as the world gives, do I give to you. Let not your heart be troubled, nor let it be fearful.' " The Lord did not want His followers to be cowards as they contemplated what it would be like without Him on earth. They had no need to be cowardly, because He promised to be with them always, even though He would be physically absent.

Deilos is translated "timid" and "cowardly" in its three occurrences in the New Testament. Matthew 8:26 says, "And he said to them, 'Why are you timid *[deilos]*, you men of little faith?' Then He arose, and rebuked the winds and the sea; and it became perfectly calm." Mark 4:40 also uses this word: " 'Why are you so timid *[deilos]*? How is it that you have no faith?" Revelation 21:8 tells of the final destiny of those who reject Jesus Christ as Savior: "But for the cowardly *[deilos]* and unbelieving and abominable and murderers and immoral persons and sorcerers and idolaters and all liars, their part will be in the lake that burns with fire and brimstone, which is the second death."

None of these Greek words is used in a positive way in the New Testament. All of them denote cowardice. Therefore, Paul was able to assure Timothy that this kind of fear does not come from the Lord. It is one thing to be afraid when there is a justifiable cause, but it is quite another thing to let fear control one's entire life. This is cowardice and does not originate with God.

Above all, the Christian should not be afraid of new circumstances, for he serves the "Christ of every crisis." Certainly the child of God will not be without fear when there is reason to fear; but he should not let fear dominate his life. His confidence will be in God.

The Old Testament experiences of the Israelites were written "for our instruction" (1 Corinthians 10:11). One of the key experiences of these people was at Kadesh-barnea, where they sent twelve spies into Canaan to see what the land was like. When the spies returned, ten of them gave a negative report on the Israelites' chances of gaining control of the land. These spies said, " 'We are not able to go up against the people, for they are too strong for us' " (Numbers 13:31). Because these ten were concentrating more on the circumstances than on God, they did not think there was any possibility that the Israelites could take the land.

The other two spies, Joshua and Caleb, trusted God and His ability to fulfill His promises. They concentrated more on God than on the circumstances, and Caleb spoke for both of them when he said, " 'We should by all means go up and take possession of it, for we shall surely overcome it' " (v. 30).

The attitude of the ten spies did not originate with God, because it was one of cowardice. They refused to believe God.

Often the reason for our reluctance about doing God's will is that we think more about circumstances than about God. When this happens, we yield to the same unbelief and cowardice as did the ten spies. This fear does not come from God. Let us, rather, have the fearless faith of Joshua and Caleb, who had confidence that their God was greater than the circumstances they faced.

35
Peace: God's Umpire

One of the significant verses that tell Christians how to know the will of God is Colossians 3:15. On the surface, the verse does not seem so crucial to the subject, because its force does not come through in many English translations. This verse states, "And let the peace of Christ rule in your hearts, to which indeed you were called in one body; and be thankful."

The Greek word that is translated "rule" in this verse is *brabeuō*. Colossians 3:15 is the only place where this word occurs in the Greek New Testament. During New Testament times *brabeuō* was used in secular literature when describing court proceedings and athletic contests. The word emphasized a decision, such as one made by the court or by an umpire. *Brabeuō* means "to arbitrate, decide, to act as an umpire." With this in mind, it is easy to see how "rule" is a good translation of the Greek word. The decision of the court and the decision of the umpires would rule in their respective areas of authority.

Applying the significance of this word to Colossians 3:15, we better understand how the Lord's will can be determined. We are to let the peace of God "act as umpire" in our hearts. Whenever we have an inner dispute about what we should do, God's peace should be the arbitrator.

God never directs His children to do something that is contrary to His written Word. Therefore, Christians should diligently study the Bible to know if a certain thing is wrong according to the Scriptures. Sometimes the most difficult matter in the Christian life is not choosing between things that are definitely right or definitely wrong. When confronted with this decision the Christian should simply obey and do what is right. The greatest difficulty is deciding between two or more things that are right — determining what is best in contrast to what is good.

After carefully studying the portions of God's Word that deal with the problem, the Christian may realize that none of the options he faces is wrong in God's sight, yet he can do only one thing. In this situation the peace of God helps him to decide what is best. He must allow the peace of God to call the decision. His whole life should be ruled by this peace, and he should make no decisions that disturb God's peace within him.

As the child of God prays concerning his options, he will discover that the peace of God will indicate which alternative to follow. This is assuming, of course, that he wants to please Jesus Christ in everything. When this is the Christian's motive, he can be sure that the indwelling Holy Spirit will guide him by giving him the peace of God.

One may not be able to explain this peace to others or even adequately defend his decision, but he can be confident that he has chosen that which is pleasing to God. That this peace is inexplainable is stated in Philippians 4:6-7: "Be anxious for nothing, but in everything by prayer and supplication with thanksgiving let your requests be made known to God. And the peace of God, which surpasses all comprehension, shall guard your hearts and your minds in Christ Jesus." Often the Christian cannot understand or explain God's peace, because God is infinite and man is finite. The marvel is not only that the infinite God has given us a revelation of Himself through the Bible but also that He communicates to us by means of peace.

Christians need to be sensitive to sin and to present themselves unreservedly to do God's will. When this is the case, the Spirit of God will use the Word of God to produce the peace of God in their lives.

36
Persistence Isn't Enough

The Greek word *akribōs* and its other forms are often translated "diligent," or "diligently" in some translations. The English word "diligent" is commonly used to mean "persistent." One who does not give up but continues to work on a task is a "diligent" person.

Though *akribōs* includes the idea of diligence, there is an even finer shade of meaning to this word and its other forms — the basic meaning is that of accuracy, or exactness. It is an accuracy which is the outcome of carefulness.

When the Wise Men came from the east to Jerusalem, looking for the one who was born King of the Jews, Herod called them aside privately and "ascertained *[akribōs]* from them the time the star appeared" (Matthew 2:7). Herod was careful to find out exactly when these men first saw the star in the east. After questioning the Wise Men, Herod "sent them to Bethlehem, and said, 'Go and make careful *[akribōs]* search for the Child' " (v. 8). Herod was concerned not only that the Wise Men should persistently search for the young Child but also that they should search accurately, or exactly, to make sure that He was the precise Child they were looking for. Herod was already plotting to destroy this rival King, and he wanted to be sure to eliminate the right person.

When the Wise Men did not return to Herod with their report, he became exceedingly angry and "sent and slew all the male children who were in Bethlehem and in all its environs, from two years old and under, according to the time which he had ascertained *[akribōs]* from the magi" (v. 16). This verse refers to Herod's careful questioning of the Wise Men, as mentioned in verse 7.

The word *akribōs* is also used of Apollos: "This man had been instructed in the way of the Lord; and being fervent in spirit, he was speaking and teaching accurately *[akribōs]* the things concerning Jesus" (Acts 18:25). Apollos was able to speak and teach the things of the Lord accurately because he was "mighty in the Scriptures" (v. 24). It is possible to persistently speak and teach the things of the Lord without being "mighty in the Scriptures," but such a ministry cannot be conducted with accuracy.

The use of the word *akribōs* did not mean that Apollos knew everything. The last phrase of verse 25 describes him as "acquainted only with the baptism of John," which indicates that he had not heard about the coming of the Holy Spirit on the day of Pentecost. Apollos did not have all the Scriptures available to him; however, he was an able, or capable, student of the Scriptures he had. When Aquila and Priscilla heard Apollos speak, they realized that he needed more information, and "they took him aside and explained to him the way of God more accurately *[akribōs]*" (v. 26). He already had quite an accurate knowledge about the way of God, but when Aquila and Priscilla shared with him additional information, he learned and was able to speak and to teach even more accurately.

This use of the word *akribos* is also seen in Acts 24:22. The apostle Paul had given his defense, but "Felix, having a more exact *[akribōs]* knowledge of the Way, put them off." Before Paul gave his defense, Felix already knew with some accuracy about Paul and the "Way" he represented; but when Paul concluded his defense, Felix knew more exactly Paul's beliefs.

The word *akribōs* is also used of believers. Ephesians 5:15 says, "Therefore be careful *[akribōs]* how you walk, not as unwise men, but as wise." The apostle Paul used the word *akribōs* when referring to the knowledge of the Thessalonian believers concerning Christ's second coming. Paul told them, "For you yourselves know full well *[akribōs]* that the day of the Lord will come just like a thief in the night" (1 Thessalonians 5:2). It was because the Thessalonian believers had an accurate knowledge concerning the second coming of the Lord that Paul told them, "Now as to the times and the epochs, brethren, you have no need of anything to be written to you" (v. 1).

Because of their accurate knowledge of the coming of the Lord, they should not be taken by surprise. While some would be taken by surprise and would not escape, Paul told his readers, "But you, brethren, are not in darkness, that the day should overtake you like a thief" (v. 4).

If we are to have an accurate knowledge about the Lord Jesus Christ and are to be able to speak and teach accurately concerning Him, it is essential that we be "mighty in the Scriptures," as was Apollos (Acts 18:24).

37
God's Justice Satisfied

When man was created, he was placed in the Garden of Eden and was told that he could freely eat of the fruit of every tree except the tree of the knowledge of good and evil (Genesis 2:16-17). Did he choose God's way or his own way? Man's first sin was that of asserting his will over God's will.

Ever since the first man sinned, the sin nature has been passed on to every descendant. Romans 5:12 refers to this fact: "Therefore, just as through one man sin entered into the world, and death through sin, and so death spread to all men, because all sinned." The greatest proof that every person is a sinner is that he will eventually die. If there had been no sin, there would be no death.

There are two aspects of man's death — physical and spiritual. Physical death occurs when the soul and spirit are separated from the body, and spiritual death occurs when the soul and spirit are separated from God. Sin has already separated every person from God; because of sin, every person born into the world is in a state of condemnation. The question is, How can a person be delivered from condemnation?

Mankind is under God's condemnation because God is perfectly righteous and cannot condone any sin. Yet, because man is hopeless in his state of sin, it is necessary for God to act on man's behalf if man is to be delivered from condemnation. But here the problem arises: How can a perfectly holy God justify, or declare righteous, a sinner? God's perfect righteousness demands justice, but the good news is that God's perfect love provides a way for mercy to be poured out on every sinner.

Referring to Jesus Christ, the apostle John said, "He Himself is the propitiation for our sins; and not for ours only, but also for those of the whole world" (1 John 2:2). The Greek word translated "propitiation" is *hilasmos*. This word means "an appeasing," or "a means of appeasing." When Jesus Christ died on the cross for sinners, His death appeased, or completely satisfied, the heavenly Father's demands concerning man's sin. Since Jesus Christ took on Himself the form of a man and died on the cross for the sins of the world, God was able to remain completely just, yet He was also able to justify those who believe in Jesus.

Hilasmos is translated the same way in 1 John 4:10: "In this is love, not that we loved God, but that He loved us and sent His Son to be the propitiation *[hilasmos]* for our sins."

A similar Greek word, *hilastērion,* is translated "mercy seat" in Hebrews 9:5: "And above it were the cherubim of glory overshadowing the mercy seat." In the Old Testament, the mercy seat in the Tabernacle, and later in the Temple, was sprinkled with atoning blood on the Day of Atonement. This act signified that the law had been carried out and *hilastērion* refers to the place of propitiation. This word also occurs in Romans 3:25, where it is translated "propitiation": "Whom [Christ] God displayed publicly as a propitiation in His blood through faith. This was to demonstrate His righteousness, because in the forbearance of God He passed over the sins previously committed."

On the cross, Christ was both the place of the propitiation and the propitiation itself. He satisfied the demands of God's justice: "For the demonstration, I say, of His righteousness at the present time, that He might be just and the justifier of the one who has faith in Jesus" (v. 26). Observe from this verse that only those who believe in Jesus are justified.

Another related Greek word, *hilaskomai,* occurs in Hebrews 2:17: "Therefore, He had to be made like His brethren in all things, that He might become a merciful and faithful high priest in things pertaining to God, to make propitiation for the sins of the people." Here, *hilaskomai* is translated "to make propitiation for." Mankind had been separated from God since Adam first sinned. Jesus' death on the cross, however, made it possible for man to be reconciled to God, because Jesus Christ propitiated (satisfied) the Father for sin.

Hilaskomai also appears in Luke 18:13: " 'But the tax-gatherer, standing some distance away, was even unwilling to lift up his eyes to heaven, but was beating his breast, saying, "God, be merciful [*hilaskomai*] to me, the sinner!" ' " Jesus had not yet died on the cross when the publican prayed this prayer. He actually prayed that God would be propitiated for his sin. This is a prayer that does not need to be prayed now, because Christ has died on the cross and has fully met the demands of God's justice.

God has done everything that needs to be done for the sinner. Now it is each person's responsibility to receive Jesus Christ as his personal Savior. When this is done, the benefits of Christ's death on the cross are applied to that individual. The good news of God's Word is that Christ has paid the penalty for every person's sin. All anyone has to do to be delivered from condemnation is to receive Jesus Christ as his personal Savior. Have you received Christ as your Savior?

38

The Conflict of the Faith

The Scriptures clearly present the truth that salvation is of faith, not of works. The apostle Paul wrote to believers: "For by grace you have been saved through faith; and that not of yourselves, it is the gift of God; not as a result of works, that no one should boast" (Ephesians 2:8-9).

There is no work that any person can do to contribute to his salvation. A person is saved from condemnation only by placing his faith in Jesus Christ as his personal Savior.

The Scriptures also say a great deal about the believer's living by faith. Romans 1:17 states, "But the righteous man shall live by faith." Colossians 2:6 says, "As you therefore have received Christ Jesus the Lord, so walk in Him."

The one who has received Jesus Christ as Savior is to walk by faith, not by sight. The believer must take God at His Word and live accordingly. For instance, the Bible promises, "If we confess our sins, He is faithful and righteous to forgive us our sins and to cleanse us from all unrighteousness" (1 John 1:9). The one who walks by faith does not depend on his feelings to tell him when he is forgiven of sin; he depends on the Word of God.

Although the believer has salvation and is to live by faith, this does not mean there is no conflict in the Christian life. Salvation is not attained by struggle but by faith, but there is a conflict which results when one places his faith in Christ.

The apostle Paul wrote about the conflict he experienced because of the Christian faith. The Greek word he used when referring to this struggle is *agōnizomai,* the word from which we get "agonize." *Agōnizomai* is used seven times in the Greek New Testament. Two of these times it is translated by a form of the word "strive" (Luke 13:24; Colossians 1:29). It appears as "competes" once (1 Corinthians 9:25). One of its occurrences is translated "laboring earnestly" (Colossians 4:12). Three times it is translated by a form of the word "fight" (John 18:36; 1 Timothy 6:12; 2 Timothy 4:7).

In Paul's time, *agōnizomai* and its related words had to do with those who participated in athletic and gladiatorial contests. Thus, it referred to those who were expending all their energies trying to win the prize. Paul brought this word into a Christian context when he applied it to serving the Lord. Paul put forth all his mental and physical energies in serving the Lord, and he exhorted others to do likewise.

To the young pastor Timothy, Paul wrote: "Fight the good fight of faith" (1 Timothy 6:12). This phrase might even be translated, "Struggle the good struggle of the faith." This phrase is even more meaningful when the context is considered. Paul had just exhorted Timothy, "But flee from these things, you man of God; and pursue righteousness, godliness, faith, love, perseverence and gentleness" (v. 11). Like everyone else, Timothy could acquire salvation only by placing faith in Christ, which he had already done. Much discipline and struggling were necessary, however, if Timothy were to excel in being what he ought to be and in doing the work of the Lord.

The apostle Paul later wrote to Timothy: "I have fought *[agōnizomai]* the good fight" (2 Timothy 4:7). As Paul, facing death, wrote these words from prison, he was able to reflect on his life and consider it as already having been finished; thus, he said, "I have finished the course, I have kept the faith" (v. 7).

Although Paul knew the rest of faith, which comes to one who realizes what he has in Jesus Christ, he did not decrease the amount of energy he was expending in getting out the gospel to others and in suffering for the cause of Christ.

No striving or struggling will cause us to be accepted by God, because we are accepted by Him only on the basis of faith (2 Corinthians 5:9). However, once we have placed our faith in Jesus Christ as Savior — and in all the resources He makes available for daily living — there is a conflict that follows as we expend our energies in glorifying Him and as we seek to win and teach others.

39
Digging Your Own Treasures

The Bible is the greatest book that has ever been written. It is God's words in written form. Our salvation depends upon whether or not we believe — and act on — the truths found in the Bible. Our spiritual growth depends upon the application of those truths in our lives. So it is important that we know what the Bible says and what it means. This involves a study of the individual words used in the Bible.

One of the problems one faces in the study of words is that meanings change according to how they are used. Another is time — the last book of the Bible was written about nineteen centuries ago. Also, the Bible was written in languages most of us do not know and in a culture with which we are not familiar. One can see why *study* is necessary to determine the meanings of words used in Bible times.

This chapter will focus on how to do a word study. But before doing that it should be emphasized that it is the nature of language that a specific word takes on different meanings from its given context. One should never establish the meaning of a word, then force the context to fit the meaning.

One cannot underestimate the importance of knowing the context as thoroughly as possible. One of the best ways to do this is by reading and rereading a particular portion until one understands how it fits into the larger whole.

Fortunately, many tools are available today to assist one in the study of individual words. Most Bible study aids of the past were based on the King James Version (KJV), but there are several helps based on some of the modern-language versions. Inasmuch as *Treasures from the Original* has employed the *New American Standard Bible* (NASB) as its primary text, the following study will begin with it.

Serious Bible study demands a concordance to trace every occurrence of a word that appears in the Bible. Such a concordance is the *New American Standard Exhaustive Concordance of the Bible*. This volume also includes Hebrew, Aramaic, and Greek dictionaries.

Let us assume that you have a question about the first part of Acts 1:8, which states: "You shall receive power when the Holy Spirit has come upon you." Perhaps you wonder, What does the word "power" mean?

Using the concordance to the NASB, look up the word "power." Under this heading, go down the list until you find the reference. Notice the number that is printed alongside the reference: "1411."

At the back of the concordance is a section entitled "Greek Dictionary of the New American Standard Exhaustive Concordance." (Follow the instructions describing the use of this section.) The words are listed according to the numbers found in the main part of the concordance. Proceed to number 1411; you find the Greek word followed by its English transliteration, *dunamis*. The following information is then given: ". . . from 1410; (miraculous) power, might, strength — ability (4), meaning (1), mightily (1), mighty (1), miracle (2), miracles (17), miraculous powers (3), power (80), Power (3), powers (6), strength (2), wealth (m)(1)."

The description indicates it is derived from the previously listed word (which is the verb form; *dunamis* is the noun form). The basic meaning or definition is given in italics, followed by the different ways (and number of times) this one Greek word *(dunamis)* is translated in the NASB. Glancing at this list gives you an idea of the shades of meaning of the word translated "power" in Acts 1:8.

(See chapter 2 for a discussion of this word.)

The numbers that appear in the concordance to the NASB are the same numbers used in *Strong's Exhaustive Concordance*, which is based on the KJV. So any Bible study aid that is keyed to the numbers in Strong's concordance to the KJV can also be used with the numbers in the NASB concordance. There is usually a difference in the English words used in the different translations, but the Greek word which appears with the number is the same.

In addition to Strong's concordance to the KJV, there is also *Young's Analytical Concordance*. I have personally found Young's to be better for the type of word study I am suggesting. For instance, as you look up the word "power" in Young's, you will find verses listed according to which Greek word for "power" is used. After locating the word "power," look down the column of references until you find "Acts 1:8." Notice that this is found under the heading *"Ability, power, dunamis* [Greek word]." Also, that the basic meaning of the word is given with the listing, which immediately gives you the shade of meaning of the word. Under this heading, all the verses are listed that use "power" to translate this one Greek word in the KJV.

If you would like to see the other ways the KJV translates *dunamis,* turn to the back section called "Index-Lexicon to the New Testament." Here the words are listed by their English transliterations. Locate *dunamis* and under this heading you will find "ability 1, abundance (M. power) 1, meaning 1, might 4, mighty deed 1, mighty work 11 . . ." The number indicates the times this word is used to translate *dunamis* in the KJV. By looking up each one of these translations in the main part of the concordance, you could trace every occurrence of this Greek word even though you have not studied Greek.

An excellent work for finding more information on individual words is *An Expository Dictionary of New Testament Words,* by W. E. Vine. Under "power," a list of and comments on all the Greek words (transliterated into English) that are translated "power" in the KJV is provided.

Commentaries written by those who know the original languages are also important to Bible study. Since the same commentary does not appeal to everyone, it is best to read a portion of the commentary first to make sure it will be of value before purchasing it. Don't spend money on books — no matter how good they are — if you won't use them. As Warren W. Wiersbe says, "It is not necessary for a library to be large to be effective. Better to have fewer of the best books than to clutter your shelves with volumes that cannot serve you well."*

For a list of books that can be of much help to you in studying the Bible, see "Recommended Tools" following this chapter. The books recommended are not expected to be accumulated in a short span of time, but they should be considered when building a strong library.

It must always be remembered that Bible study is *study*. You will be greatly pleased, however, and you will grow spiritually by the gems you discover as you dig out your own treasures from the original.

* Warren W. Wiersbe, *Listening to the Giants* (Grand Rapids: Baker, 1979), p. 270.

Recommended Tools

BASIC LEVEL

ATLAS

Beitzel, Barry J. *The Moody Atlas of Bible Lands*. Chicago: Moody, 1985.
Pfeiffer, Charles F. *Baker's Bible Atlas*. Grand Rapids: Baker, 1961.

COMMENTARY

Harrison, Everett F., and Pfeiffer, Charles, eds. *Wycliffe Bible Commentary*. Chicago: Moody, 1962.

CONCORDANCE

Cruden, Alexander. *Cruden's Complete Concordance*. Grand Rapids: Zondervan, 1949.

DICTIONARY

Unger, Merrill F. *Unger's Bible Dictionary*. 3d ed. Chicago: Moody, 1966.

ENCYCLOPEDIA

Pfeiffer, Charles F.; Vos, Howard F.; and Rea, John, eds. *Wycliffe Bible Encyclopedia*. 2 vols. Chicago: Moody, 1975.

SURVEY

Gromacki, Robert G. *New Testament Survey.* Grand Rapids: Baker, 1979.

ADVANCED LEVEL

COMMENTARIES

Vincent, Marvin R. *Word Studies in the New Testament.* 4 vols. Grand Rapids: Eerdmans, 1957.

Walvoord, John F., and Zuck, Roy B., eds. *Bible Knowledge Commentary.* Wheaton, Ill.: Victor, 1983.

Wuest, Kenneth S. *Word Studies in the Greek New Testament.* 3 vols. Grand Rapids: Eerdmans, 1969.

CONCORDANCES

Strong, James. *Strong's Exhaustive Concordance.* Nashville:Abingdon, 1980.

Thomas, Robert L., ed. *New American Standard Exhaustive Concordance of the Bible.* Nashville: Holman, 1981.

Young, Robert. *Young's Analytical Concordance to the Bible.* Grand Rapids: Eerdmans, 1955.

DICTIONARIES

Blaiklock, E. M., and Harrison, R. K., eds. *New International Dictionary of Biblical Archaeology.* Grand Rapids: Zondervan, 1983.

Vine, W. E. *An Expository Dictionary of New Testament Words.* Chicago, Moody, 1985.

ENCYCLOPEDIA

Tenney, Merrill C., ed. *Zondervan Pictorial Encyclopedia of the Bible.* 5 vols. Grand Rapids: Zondervan, 1979.

INTRODUCTION

Thiessen, Henry C. *Introduction to the New Testament*. Grand Rapids: Eerdmans, 1943.

GREEK HELPS

COMMENTARIES

Gaebelein, Frank E., ed. *Expositor's Bible Commentary*. 6 vols. Grand Rapids: Zondervan, 1980.

Lenski, R. C. H. *New Testament Commentary*. 12 vols. Minneapolis: Augsburg.

Robertson, Archibald T. *Word Pictures in the New Testament*. 6 vols. Nashville: Broadman, 1981.

CONCORDANCE

Wigram, George V. *Englishman's Greek Concordance of the New Testament*. Grand Rapids: Zondervan, 1979.

DICTIONARY

Brown, Colin, ed. *New International Dictionary of New Testament Theology*. 3 vols. Grand Rapids: Zondervan, 1975-78.

GRAMMARS

Dana, H. E., and Mantey, J. R. *Manual Grammar of the Greek New Testament*. New York: Macmillan, 1957. (Advanced)

Summers, Ray. *Essentials of New Testament Greek*. Nashville: Broadman, 1950. (Beginner)

GREEK TESTAMENT

Interlinear Greek-English New Testament (various publishers).

LEXICONS

Bauer, Walter, ed. *Greek-English Lexicon of the New Testament*. trans. William R. Arndt and F. Wilbur Gingrich. Grand Rapids: Zondervan, 1979.

Gingrich, F. Wilbur. *Shorter Lexicon of the New Testament.* Grand Rapids: Zondervan, 1983.

PARSING/READING HELPS Han, E. S. *Parsing Guide to the Greek New Testament.* Scottsdale, Pa.: Herald, 1971.

Kubo, Sakae. *Reader's Greek-English Lexicon of the New Testament.* Grand Rapids: Zondervan, 1975.

Moulton, Harold K. *Analytical Greek Lexicon to the New Testament.* Grand Rapids: Zondervan, 1979.

WORD STUDIES Moulton, James H., and Milligan, George. *Vocabulary of the Greek New Testament.* Grand Rapids: Eerdmans, 1949.

Trench, Robert C. *Synonyms of the New Testament.* Grand Rapids: Eerdmans, 1950.

Scripture Index

Genesis
2:16-17   105

Exodus
20:14   65
23:27   97

Numbers
13:30   99
13:31   98

Joshua
15:8   19

2 Chronicles
33:1-6   19

Proverbs
9:10   97

Isaiah
57:21   37

Jeremiah
7:31   19

Matthew
2:7   102-3
2:8   102
2:16   103
3:2   48
4:3   46
4:7   46
5:10-12   63
5:22   18
5:28   65
5:29   18
5:30   18
6:2   67-68
6:5   68
6:16   68
8:26   97-98
10:28   18
11:23   18
13:52   33

16:16   14
16:18   18
16:19   14-15
18:9   18
18:18   14-15
23:15   18
23:33   18
25:41   20
25:46   20
26:55   22
27:3-5   50
27:57   33
28:19   32-33

Mark
1:19   54
4:18-19   66
4:23   60
4:40   97-98
9:42-50   19
9:43   18
9:44   19

9:45	18	**John**		18:24	103-4	
9:46	19	1:11-12	49	18:25	103	
9:47	18	1:12	6	18:26	103	
9:48	19	2:16	57	19:27	21	
12:35	22	2:19	23	22:3	88	
16:12	24	2:21	23	24:22	103	
16:15	33	3:5-6	11			
		3:16-18	20	**Romans**		
Luke		5:24	20, 31, 49,	1:9	38	
1:9	22		63, 90	1:16	57	
1:10	22	5:37	70	1:17	108	
1:19	84	8:44	66	1:31	73	
2:1	35	13:35	87	2:20	89	
2:7	35	14:16	77	3:3	2	
2:8	36	14:26	77-78	3:25	106	
2:9	36	15:26	77-78	3:26	106	
2:10	36	16:7	77-78	5:5-6	73	
2:11	36	16:7-11	11-13	5:12	105	
2:12	36	16:8	11	6:6	1	
2:13-14	37	16:8-11	78	6:6-10	83	
2:18-19	37	16:9	12	6:11	42-44	
2:51	27	16:11	13	6:11-12	83	
3:22	70	16:12-15	78	6:13	83-84	
6:27	74	18:22	84	6:16	83	
9:29	70	18:36	109	6:19	83	
10:15	18	19:10-11	49	8:28-29	90	
10:17	27	19:24	57	9:2	39	
11:4	56-57	20:23	15	9:21	6	
12:5	18			12:1	84	
13:3	48	**Acts**		12:2	47	
13:24	109	1:8	5, 112-13	12:10	72	
16:19-31	18	2:27	18	12:13	86	
16:23	18	2:31	18			
18:13	107	5:9	46	**1 Corinthians**		
19:47	22	7:22	88	1:7	2	
22:15	64	14:21	33	2:3	57	
23:16, 22	88	18:9	57-58	3:1	2	
24:21	81	18:10	58	3:1-4	94	

3:9	93	5:7	70	2:6-7	24
3:10-11	93	5:9	110	2:7	25
3:12-13	94	5:10	94	2:8	24-25
3:16-17	23	5:17	10	3:12-14	63
4:16	92	5:21	13, 41-42	3:17	91
6:16	23	6:9	88	4:6-7	101
6:16-17	23	6:14	28		
6:19	23	6:16	23	**Colossians**	
6:19-20	23	7:31	24	1:21-23	60
6:20	80	8:3	4	1:29	109
7:23	80	9:4	75	2:6	108
8:1	94	11:17	75	2:20	60
8:10	94	13:5	46	3:1	61
8:12	95			3:2	61
9:6	5	**Galatians**		3:15	100
9:25	109	1:9	16	4:5	81
10:11	98	2:20	15, 42-43	4:12	109
10:13	46	3:13	81		
10:23	95	4:5	81	**1 Thessalonians**	
11:1	92	5:16	3, 53, 66	1:2	39
11:3	28	5:17	66	1:3	38
11:32	88	5:22-23	53	1:6-7	92
13:8	2	5:25	53	2:13	39
13:10	2	5:26	54	2:17	66
14:3-4	95	6:1	54-55	5:1	104
14:5	95			5:2	104
14:12	95	**Ephesians**		5:4	104
14:17	96	2:8	15	5:17	39
14:20	51	2:8-9	6, 108	5:21-22	71
14:26	96	5:15	103	5:22	70
14:32	27	5:16	81		
14:34	27	5:25	28	**2 Thessalonians**	
15:30	43	6:4	88	3:8-9	92
15:31	43-44				
15:34	43	**Philippians**		**1 Timothy**	
		1:23	66	1:20	88
2 Corinthians		2:5	24	3:2	87
4:4	13	2:6	24	6:11	109

6:12	109	12:10	88	3:5	12
		12:11	88	3:6	7-9
2 Timothy		13:2	87	3:6-9	7-8
1:3	39			3:7	8
1:7	97	**James**		3:8	9
2:13	2	1:2	45	3:9	7, 9
2:22	62	1:3-4	52	4:7-8	73
2:25	88	1:12	45-46	4:10	106
3:3	73	1:13	45-46, 57		
3:16	88	3:6	18	**Revelation**	
4:7	109			1:8	18
		1 Peter		3:19	88
Titus		1:5	5	5:9	81
1:7-8	87	1:7	47, 71, 90	6:8	18
2:5	27	2:18	27	6:16-17	31
2:9	27	3:1	26, 28	11:18	31
2:12	88	3:5	26	14:10	30-31
2:14	82	3:6	28	14:19	30
		4:8	87	15:1	30
Hebrews		4:9	87	15:7	30
1:3	75	5:2-3	92	16:1	30
2:17	106			16:19	30-31
3:14	75	**2 Peter**		18:3	30
5:14	52	2:4	17	19:15	30-31
9:5	106	3:9	20	19:20	19
11:1	75-76			20:10	19
12:5	88	**1 John**		20:11-15	19, 31
12:5-11	89	1:9	3, 8, 108	20:13	18
12:6	88	2:1	8, 79	20:13-15	18
12:7	88	2:2	20, 36, 49,	20:14	18
12:8	88		79, 106	20:15	19
12:9	89	2:16	66	21:8	97, 98

Greek Word Index

adialeiptos, 38 39
agapē, 73-74
agonizomai, 109
agorazō, 80-81
akribōs, 102-3
allos, 78
apechō, 67
astorgē, 73

brabeuō, 100

deilaō, 97
deilia, 97
deilos, 97-98
diōkō, 62-63, 86
dokimazō, 47, 71
dunamis, 4-5, 112

eidos, 70-71
eleēmosunē, 67
elegchō, 12

epithumeō, 65-66
epithumia, 65-66
eros, 72
euaggelizomai, 36
exagorazō, 80-81
exousia, 4-6

geenna, 17 20

hadēs, 17-18, 20
hieron, 21-23
hilaskomai, 106-7
hilasmos, 106
hilastērion, 106
hupostasis, 75-76
hupotassō, 26-27

katargeō, 1-2
katartizō, 54

lutroō, 80-82

mathēteuō, 32-33
metamelomai, 50
metanoeō, 48
mimētēs, 92
morphē, 24-25

naos, 21-23

oikodomē, 93, 95
oikodomeō, 93-96
oikoumenē, 35
orgē, 29-31

paideia, 88-89
paideuō, 88-89
paideutēs, 88-89
paraklētos, 77-79
paristēmi, 84
peirasmos, 45-46
peirazō, 45-47
philos, 73

philoxenia, 86
philoxenos, 87

schēma, 24-25
storgē, 72-73

tartaroō, 17
tartaros, 17, 20
teleioō, 51
teleios, 51-52
thumos, 29-31
tupos, 91-92

New American Standard Bible *Word Index*

Abide, 9
Ability, 4, 112
Accurately, 103
Advocate, 79
Alive, 42-43
Alms, 67
Anger, 31
Another, 77-78
Appearance, 25
Ascertained, 102-3
Assurance, 75-76

Baptize, 33
Be devoted to, 73
Bind, 15
Build, 94
Building, 93
Bought, 80

Careful, 102-3
Compete, 109

Confidence, 75
Confidence of
    boasting, 75
Constantly, 39
Convict, 12
Correct, 88
Corrector, 89
Cowardly, 98
Crucified, 42

Dead, 42
Desire, 65-66
Disciple, 32-33
Discipline, 88-89
Done away, 1-2

Edification, 95-96
Edify, 94-96
Educate, 88
Examine, 71
Example, 91-92

Fierce, 30-31
Fight, 109
Fire, 19
Flee, 62
Forgiven, 16
Form, 24-25, 71
Full well, 103

Go, 93

Have, 67
Hell, 17
Helper, 77-78
Hospitable, 87
Hospitality, 86-87

If, 60
Imitator, 92
Inhabited earth,
    35
Instruct, 88

Laboring earnestly, 109
Loose, 15
Love, 73
Lust, 65

Making the most, 81
Mature, 51-52
Meaning, 112
Meekness, 54
Mending, 54
Merciful, 107
Mercy seat, 106
Mightily, 112
Mighty, 112
Miracle, 112
Miraculous powers, 112
More exact, 103

Passion, 30
Perfect, 52
Power, 5, 112-13
Practice, 8-9, 86

Present, 84
Propitiation, 106
Punish, 88
Purchase, 81
Pursue, 62

Redeem, 81-82
Remorse, 50
Repent, 48
Restore, 53-54
Retain, 16
Reward in full, 67-68
Right, 5-6
Rule, 100

Sanctuary, 23
Sin, 8-9
Spiritual, 53
Stand, 84
Standing by, 84
Strengthen, 94
Strive, 109
Subject, 27
Submissive, 26, 28

Teach, 33-34, 88
Temple, 21-22
Tempt, 45
Test, 46-47
Timid, 98
To discipline, 89
To make propitiation for, 107
Train, 88
Trial, 45
Trying them out, 47

Unceasingly, 38
Unloving, 73

Was educated, 88
Will test, 47
Without ceasing, 38-39
Wrath, 30-31

Yield, 83

Moody Press, a ministry of Moody Bible Institute, is designed for education, evangelization, and edification. If we may assist you in knowing more about Christ and the Christian life, please write us without obligation: Moody Press, c/o MLM, Chicago, Illinois 60610.